Policing Matters

Equality and Diversity in Policing

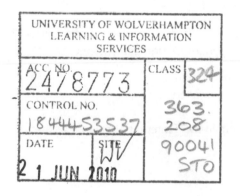

Brian Stout

Series editors

P A J Waddington

Martin Wright

LearningMatters

First published in 2010 by Learning Matters Ltd

British Library Cataloguing in Publication Data
A CIP record for this book is available from the British Library.

ISBN: 978 1 84445 353 5

This book is also available in the following ebook formats:

Adobe ebook   ISBN: 978 1 84445 665 9
EPUB ebook   ISBN: 978 1 84445 664 2
Kindle   ISBN: 978 1 84445 973 5

Cover design by Toucan Design
Project Management by Diana Chambers
Typeset by Kelly Winter
Printed and bound in Great Britain by TJ International Ltd, Padstow, Cornwall

Learning Matters Ltd
33 Southernhay East
Exeter EX1 1NX
Tel: 01392 215560
info@learningmatters.co.uk
www.learningmatters.co.uk

All weblinks and web addresses in the book have been carefully checked prior to publication, but for up-to-date information please visit the Learning Matters website, www.learningmatters.co.uk.

FSC
Mixed Sources
Product group from well-managed
forests and other controlled sources

Cert no. SGS-COC-2482
www.fsc.org
© 1996 Forest Stewardship Council

Contents

v

1 Getting started

BOOK OBJECTIVES

By the end of this book you should be able to:

- outline the key national policy and legislation that relate to all six strands of diversity and that are relevant to policing;
- describe at an introductory level some of the historical, criminological and sociological context relating to policing and all six strands of diversity;
- demonstrate knowledge of past and present police practice in relation to all six strands of diversity and show an ability to implement best practice in the future;
- reflect on the issues in dealing with particular sorts of offending, such as hate crime.

LINKS TO STANDARDS

This introductory chapter provides opportunities for links with the following Skills for Justice, National Occupational Standards (NOS) for Policing and Law Enforcement 2008.

AE1.1   Maintain and develop your own knowledge, skills and competence.
CA1   Use law enforcement actions in a fair and justified way.
HA1   Manage your own resources.
HA2   Manage your own resources and professional development.

Links to current NOS will be provided at the start of each chapter; however, it should be noted that these are subject to review and it is recommended that you visit the Skills for Justice website to check the currency of all the NOS provided: www.skillsforjustice-nosfinder.com.

Introduction

This book will cover the issues of equality and diversity in the police. Working with diversity goes to the heart of the function of a police officer, and the responsibility to serve the whole community. This book, it is hoped, will make a contribution to achieving the aim of diversity training as identified by Bryant et al.:

The aim of diversity training within the police service is usually to help you to meet the expectations of the public you serve and of your organisation regarding your attitude and behaviour towards other people and members of diverse communities.

(2006, p63)

As such, diversity training for police officers needs to go beyond simply training officers to do what the law requires. It should also lead to them internalising the messages of the training and respecting diversity because of their acceptance that it is the right thing to do.

The introduction will set out some general arguments as to why equality and diversity are important for society and for the police, and will cover some of the history of and background to the ways in which the police work with diversity. It will focus in particular on the changes in society and changes in policing since the Lawrence Inquiry and the coming into office of the Labour government in 1997.

The book is structured to allow consideration of the six strands of diversity, with one chapter devoted to each. The chapter on race, Chapter 5, acknowledges the difficult history that the police have had with regard to racism and race relations. The writing of this book coincides with the tenth anniversary of the publication of the Macpherson Inquiry report on the death of Stephen Lawrence, and Chapter 5 considers the impact of this report and how it has changed policing. Chapter 6, on religion, pays particular attention to policing in Northern Ireland and the work towards creating a non-sectarian police force that commands the confidence of all sections of the community. Chapter 4, on gender, discusses the role and influence of women police officers and the difficult history of, and improving current practice in, the investigation of sexual and violent crimes against women. This is followed by the chapter on sexual orientation, Chapter 7, which traces the journey that the police service has made from being considered hostile to the gay community to now being identified as one of the model employers. The chapter on disability, Chapter 3, deals with the response of the police to the need to make reasonable adjustments for employees with disabilities, as well as the important issue of the policing of disability hate crime. The last of the six strands of diversity is age and the chapter on this subject, Chapter 2, looks at both the response of the police to age discrimination legislation and the approach of the police and the criminal justice system as a whole to crime committed by young people.

All chapters follow a similar format, and initially set the objectives of the chapter and identify the legislative and policy context. This is followed by some discussion of criminological and sociological approaches to the diversity strand in question. The reason for doing this is twofold. First, it is helpful to put the police response to aspects of diversity in theoretical and societal context. There is much in the history of the police's response to diversity that now appears to be very poor practice. It is helpful to contextualise this by considering how broader society also struggled with some of these issues. Second, many students of policing study the subject alongside criminology or on programmes that have pathways into and out of criminology programmes. It is useful therefore to draw these links. After the discussion of criminology, the chapters go on to discuss past and present police practice, followed by some examples of best current practice and ideas for the future. The police, nationally and locally, are setting very high standards for themselves in working with diversity in the future and it is useful to set these out.

This book is an introductory text, and throughout the book the primary sources from where material is taken is identified and each chapter signposts the reader to further sources, both books and websites. There are also practical and reflective tasks in each chapter. These can be undertaken individually, but most are best carried out as tasks for learning sets or seminar groups, so that you can work together with other students to learn from each other, as well as from the written material.

The context for discussing equality, diversity and policing is an ever-changing one. This book was written in late 2009 and, during the time of writing, the Equality Bill progressed towards enactment and the death of Fiona Pilkington and Francecca Hardwick led the previously neglected issue of disability hate crime to receive national attention. Also, the failed prosecution of bed and breakfast owners, Ben and Sharon Vogelenzang, provoked further debate about the law on inciting religious hatred. In 2010, a general election and possible change of government could have significant implications for policing, but it is also likely that some unforeseen event will highlight a particular diversity issue and the police response to it will receive publicity and policy attention. It is impossible to anticipate exactly what might happen, but it is hoped that the material in this book will equip police students not just for the current environment but for the changing context to come.

REFLECTIVE TASK

Diversity and policing

- *Why is it important for police officers to be aware of and respectful towards diversity?*

- *When you think of the six strands of diversity (age, disability, gender, race, religion, sexual orientation) are there any that you are particularly looking forward to reading some more about?*

- *Are there any of the strands that either make you feel anxious or you feel are not relevant to the work of a police officer?*

Policy and legislation

The current legislation relating to each of the strands of diversity is discussed in the relevant chapters. In this section, the broader context will be set out. First, the importance of human rights and the role of the Human Rights Act will be outlined. Particular attention will be given to the responsibilities and challenges facing the police in dealing with public assemblies and gatherings. In the second section the proposed new single Equality Bill will be outlined.

Human rights

When an individual deals with the criminal justice system – whether as a victim, a witness or a defendant, he or she has the right to be treated fairly and without discrimination. The courts, police, probation and prison services are all part of the criminal justice system, which plays an important role in tackling discrimination. The courts have a central role in hearing discrimination claims and deciding on remedies when claims are successful.

PRACTICAL TASK

The Equality and Human Rights Commission

The EHRC was launched in October 2007 and replaced its predecessor organisations, the Commission for Racial Equality, the Disability Rights Commission and the Equal Opportunities Commission. These organisations focused on each strand of diversity in isolation, but the task of the EHRC is to promote fairness throughout Britain. It is tasked with promoting equality across seven strands: age, disability, gender, race, religion and belief, sexual orientation and gender reassignment.

Visit the EHRC website and familiarise yourself with its work.

One of the most important pieces of legislation relating to equality and discrimination is the Human Rights Act 1998. This Act brings into UK law the rights laid down in the European Convention on Human Rights (1953). Several of these rights are particularly relevant for the criminal justice system.

- The right to liberty and security.

- Freedom from torture and degrading treatment.

- The right to a fair trial.

- The right not to be punished for something that wasn't a crime when you did it.

- The right to respect for private and family life.

- Freedom of thought, conscience and religion.

- The right not to be discriminated against in enjoyment of these rights.

If any one of these rights or freedoms is infringed, an individual has the right to an effective resolution in law, even if the infringement was by someone in authority, such as a police officer.

In many cases, the Human Rights Act also protects against unfair treatment on grounds including, but not limited to, those of sex, race, disability, sexual orientation, religion or belief, and age. The Act allows British citizens to seek legal remedies in British courts, rather than having to go to the European Court of Human Rights.

PRACTICAL TASK

The European Court of Human Rights

The European Court of Human Rights is an international court that was set up to adjudicate on allegations of breaches of the European Convention on Human Rights. Its judgments are binding on the countries concerned. The Court was set up in 1959, so is celebrating its fiftieth anniversary in 2009. It is based in Strasbourg, France.

Visit the European Court website and familiarise yourself with its work.

In addition to the legal protection offered by human rights legislation, the criminal justice system is also subject to anti-discrimination legislation that prevents it from discriminating unlawfully against anyone on the grounds of sex, race, disability, religion or belief, age or sexual orientation.

PRACTICAL TASK

The Council of Europe

In reading about human rights nationally and internationally you will come across many references to the Council of Europe. The Council of Europe is an international organisation that promotes human rights, democracy and the rule of law. It was founded in 1948 and is based in Strasbourg, France. It pre-dates the formation of the European Economic Community and is entirely separate from it.

Visit the Council of Europe website and familiarise yourself with its work.

As public authorities, criminal justice institutions, such as the Prison Service, police forces, the National Probation Service and the Crown Prosecution Service, are also subject to certain legal duties, which require them to positively promote equality. Criminal justice institutions may also be classified as service providers, in which case they are bound by rules similar to those of other service providers. They may also be employers, and as such have certain legal responsibilities to their staff.

The promotion of human rights is highly politicised and often controversial. Opponents of the Human Rights Act argue that human rights legislation prevents the police from fighting crime; promotes the interests of groups such as prisoners, asylum seekers and travellers to the detriment of the 'majority population'; encourages a culture of litigation; and is a non-British approach that has been imposed from Europe. Even the current, at the time of writing, Justice Secretary Jack Straw, who as Home Secretary was responsible for introducing the Human Rights Act and continues strongly to support it, has been critical of how the Act is being interpreted by the courts. Straw has said that he would expect the courts to give greater weight to responsibilities as well as rights, and has suggested that a

Bill of Rights and Responsibilities might be an appropriate way to build on the Human Rights Act (Straw, 2009).

Prisoners and the right to vote

One of the highest-profile and most contentious debates relating to the Human Rights Act relates to whether prisoners should have the right to vote. The European Court of Human Rights ruled in 2004 that the UK ban on prisoners having the vote was in violation of Article 3 of the Convention and therefore unlawful. The government appealed that finding, but lost the appeal and, in December 2006, began a consultation to decide which prisoners would be allowed to vote. This consultation was followed by a second consultation, which proposed extending the right to vote to some, not all, prisoners and determining which prisoners had that right on the basis of the length of sentence imposed. At the time of writing the consultation is still open, but the government, through Justice Minister Michael Wills, is clear in stating that no prisoner serving a sentence of over four years will be permitted to vote:

> *The government has made it clear that it disagreed with the European Court of Human Rights ruling. However, the result of the ruling is that some degree of voting being extended to some serving prisoners is legally unavoidable. But, importantly, the government does not propose to give all prisoners the vote.*

> *We will ensure that, whatever the outcome of this consultation, the most serious and dangerous offenders held in custody will not be able to vote. We believe this . . . reflects the expectation of the British public that those guilty of the most serious offences should not be entitled to vote while in custody.*

> *(Ministry of Justice, 2009, no pagination)*

The government is complying reluctantly with the Court's ruling as slowly as possible and in as limited a way as possible. The Prison Reform Trust takes a very different view and is campaigning in favour of votes for prisoners:

> *Barring prisoners from voting may actually harm rehabilitation work, since participating in elections is likely to encourage them to become responsible, law-abiding citizens . . . voting rights and representation form part of the process of preparing prisoners for resettlement in their communities . . . granting prisoners the right to vote would neither threaten public safety nor be difficult to implement.*

> *(Lyon, 2009, no pagination)*

You can read about the Prison Reform Trust's campaign on their website.

- *What are your views on whether some or all serving prisoners should have the vote?*

- *What would be the advantages and disadvantages of giving prisoners the vote?*

There have been recent strong defences of the Human Rights Act from key figures in criminal justice and the police. The EHRC produced a report of the Human Rights Inquiry (EHRC, 2009a), which defended the Human Rights Act and called on the government to improve its record of promoting and defending the Act. It called for greater leadership and support for human rights and a more explicit use of human rights language. The report also suggested that public bodies (including the police) should go beyond a defensive approach to human rights and actively promote them. The general findings of the Inquiry were as follows.

- The fundamental principles of the Human Rights Act reflect traditional values of fairness and justice.

- The value of human rights is overwhelmingly accepted by society.

- Human rights are not just abstract concepts; they are an effective tool to deliver organisational success and to provide better services for the public.

The report contains a section on policing and it quotes from an Assistant Chief Constable, who describes the Act as 'both a sword and a shield' (EHRC, 2009a, p26) and says that it is effective in protecting front-line police staff as they carry out their duties:

> *For a lot of our people who are at the more critical end, human rights is part of their professional bit of kit . . . it's how they protect themselves to a certain extent. But it's also part of their pride I think in knowing what to do.*
>
> (EHRC, 2009a, p26)

The report quotes senior police staff, who state that human rights language has become a normal part of day-to-day police discourse. It also contains praise from other organisations for how the police have responded to the Human Rights Act, such as Stonewall, who told the enquiry that the police had been proactive in how they responded to homophobic hate crime.

CASE STUDY

The Osman case involves a decision of the European Court of Human Rights that probably has the greatest implications for the police. This case involved an obsessive teacher who assaulted a former pupil, Ahmet Osman, and killed his father, Ali Osman. The court found that the police had a duty to protect life where there was a foreseeable and immediate risk. The EHRC Inquiry report found that most police constabularies had policies on handling threats to life in order to comply with the Osman ruling. The Inquiry found that national policies were also in place and awareness of this case was high (EHRC, 2009a).

One of the EHRC report's authors, Nuala O'Loan, has a background in policing, as Northern Ireland Policing Ombudsman, and expanded on the message of the report with particular reference to policing (O'Loan, 2009). She argues that, for a police force to be considered legitimate and to ensure a secure and fair society, it must follow a human rights approach. As Ombudsman, O'Loan had the experience of dealing with complaints relating to the excessive use of force by the police, and she was able to observe what an alienating effect that had on the community. She said that taking a human rights approach has had a demonstrable and positive effect on policing:

> *The results in Northern Ireland of developing effective human rights-compliant policing have been significant. People are now coming forward to help police in a way that has not happened in the past. Complaints of abuse of force, intimidation and harassment by police officers fell over seven years from 52 per cent to 36 per cent of complaints. The level of compensation paid, and the number of officer days lost as a consequence of injury on duty also diminished rapidly. People and police officers are safer, and suffer less injury.*

(O'Loan, 2009, no pagination)

REFLECTIVE TASK

Legitimacy

The National Policing Improvement Agency, in giving evidence to the Human Rights Inquiry, stated:

> *If human rights are done right they can have a powerful legitimising effect. They are a key part of effectiveness in policing.*

(EHRC, 2009a, p25)

Legitimacy is defined by the Dictionary of Policing as:

> *Police legitimacy, therefore, is the belief that the police are entitled to call upon the public to comply with the law.*

(Murphy, 2009, p190)

This is broken down by Bryant et al. (2006) into consensual legitimacy – the support and consent of those being policed, and moral legitimacy – adherence to the rule of law.

- *What does it mean for a police force to be 'legitimate' and why is this important?*

- *How does following a human rights approach contribute to the legitimacy of the police?*

Another prominent figure with a background in Northern Ireland policing, former Chief Constable of the Police Service of Northern Ireland (PSNI), Hugh Orde, used the occasion of his appointment as chair of the Association of Chief Police Officers (ACPO) to state his commitment to human rights. He argued that they should be at the centre of all policing, particularly police training:

> *it makes sense to see if your policies comply with human rights and that there's no conflict. After all, every piece of legislation is tested for human rights. And we haven't been stopped doing the policing we need to do by human rights. It has helped us. If evidence is gathered in accordance with human rights principles it goes to court and is more likely to stand up.*

(quoted in Laville, 2009, no pagination)

The most vigorous defence of human rights, however, was delivered by retired senior Law Lord, Lord Bingham, at Liberty's Annual Conference (Bingham, 2009). Lord Bingham made ten points that he suggested should inform any debate on human rights.

1. The European Convention on Human Rights is not un-British. British politicians contributed to its drafting and the UK was the first country to ratify it.

2. The UK was obligated under international law to observe the convention even before the passing of the Human Rights Act.

3. The Human Rights Act did not give British citizens rights they did not have before; it simply enabled them to enforce those rights in British courts.

4. The Act did not transfer decision-making from politicians to judges. Decisions made by judges after the Act would have been made by different judges (in the European Court) before the Act.

5. The Act is not undemocratic. It was enacted with a clear democratic mandate and preserves the sovereignty of Parliament.

6. The Act does not unduly elevate the rights of the individual; it balances the rights of the individual and those of the community.

7. The Act does outline rights and not responsibilities, but our responsibilities as citizens (for example to pay taxes and to educate our children) are properly set out elsewhere.

8. The Convention provides minimum standards and does not prevent any state from going even further in promoting the rights of its citizens.

9. Although individual decisions made under the Convention are sometimes criticised, this is true for all judicial decision-making.

10. The rights protected by the Act and the Convention are those that are fundamental to human existence.

Lord Bingham summarises these rights (see the list on page 4) and then asks:

> *Which of these rights, I ask, would you wish to discard? Are any of them trivial, superfluous, unnecessary? Are any of them un-British? There may be those who would like to live in a country where these rights are not protected, but I am not of their number. Human rights are not, however, protected for the likes of people like me – or most of you. They are protected for the benefit of all of society's outcasts, those who need legal protection because they have no other voice – the prisoners, the mentally ill, the gipsies, the homosexuals, the immigrants, the asylum-seekers, those who are at any time the subject of public obloquy.*
>
> (Bingham, 2009, no pagination)

REFLECTIVE TASK

Human rights

Do you see it as being central to the role of a police officer to protect the fundamental human rights of all British citizens?

Human rights and the right to free assembly

One of the most contentious issues concerning human rights and the police relates to the right to free assembly and the police response to campaigners, protestors and marchers. This right is contained in Article 11 of the Human Rights Act, which states that everyone has the right to freedom of assembly and association. However, the Act does go on to state that this right does not prevent the police from lawfully restricting the exercise of that right.

The role of the police in monitoring, patrolling and enforcing the law when large groups of people have assembled has been extremely controversial, both before and after the introduction of the Human Rights Act. The task of the police, to protect against possible violence and disorder while allowing peaceful assembly, while all the time remaining apolitical, is an incredibly difficult one and one that they have not always succeeded in carrying out. Examples of past controversial issues related to the policing of large assemblies include the following.

- The miners' strike of the 1980s was one of the most bitter industrial disputes in recent British history. The role of the police in this strike, and the measures they took to maintain public order, led to a significant change in the way the police were perceived by the public (see Newburn, 2003).

- During the Hillsborough disaster of 1989, when 96 Liverpool football fans died, the police faced considerable criticism, both for how they managed the events on the day and for how they subsequently described the events (see Scraton, 2009).

- In Northern Ireland, the annual summer marching season leads to tensions between the Protestant and Catholic communities, and an inevitable involvement of the police. This was particularly evident at Drumcree in Portadown in 1995 and 1996 when police decisions to allow parades, despite the opposition of the Catholic community living on the route, caused great anger in the Catholic community. The institution of the Northern Ireland Parades Commission, the political progress made through the peace process and the change from the Royal Ulster Constabulary (RUC) to the Police Service of Northern Ireland (PSNI) have led to some easing of these tensions (see Mulcahy, 2006).

These are well-known and high-profile events and, although none of them is recent, they continue to have ramifications for how the police force is perceived. However, in 2009, there continued to be incidents in which the role of the police in managing large groups of people was called into question. The most prominent of these was the G20 protests in London, where the death of Ian Tomlinson led to both accusations of police misconduct on the day and allegations of a subsequent cover-up. The report of Her Majesty's Inspectorate of Constabulary, *Adapting to Protest*, was published in November 2009 (HMIC, 2009). Other incidents in 2009 that have led to similar debates include the police response to both BNP rallies and the anti-fascist protestors that often picket such rallies. Local constabularies have also attracted national attention for their response to climate change protestors who wished to demonstrate outside (and, in some cases, shut down) the power stations at Ratcliffe-upon-Soar, Didcot and Kingsnorth.

Peaceful protest

Striking a balance between the right of people to protest peacefully and the need to maintain public order is one of the most difficult tasks for the police. As with much else in policing, mistakes lead to serious and tragic consequences, but quiet competence and sensible decision-making seem to go unnoticed. Police officers responsible for monitoring large gatherings will need to respond to operational instructions, but could also bring their own assumptions, and even prejudices, to the decisions they need to make. For example, one of the criticisms levelled at the police at Hillsborough was that they treated football fans as potential hooligans, rather than law-abiding citizens seeking an after-noon's entertainment. We all have these assumptions and preconceptions and it is useful to be aware of them.

Look at each of the categories of people below, and write down the first three words that enter your mind when you think of them (be honest!).

- *Football fans*
- *Striking miners*
- *Climate change protestors*
- *Members of the BNP*
- *Anti-fascist protestors*
- *Cricket fans*
- *London Marathon runners*
- *Striking post office workers*

Have a look at what you have written; it might surprise you to see that you have some ingrained assumptions, even about groups of people that you might be a member of. How do you think these unconscious assumptions might affect operational police decisions you might take? Think particularly of your need to balance public order with the right to free assembly.

Equality and diversity: the Equality Bill

At the time of writing, legislation relating to equality and diversity is contained in a variety of different Acts, and these are introduced in the relevant chapters of this book. However, in 2009 the government proposed a single Equality Bill, to replace and update this legislation.

The government argues that a single bill is needed because, although a lot of progress has been made in seeking equality, there is a lot still to do. Examples of this include the prevalence of homophobic bullying in schools, the gender pay gap and the difficulties some people with disabilities have in finding employment. The government says that a single act is required to provide clear guidance to employers and streamline the legislation as:

- the law has grown for over 40 years, so it is complex and difficult to navigate;

- there are now nine pieces of discrimination legislation, 100 statutory instruments and over 2,500 pages of guidance.

The government outlines 11 ways in which the Equality Bill will strengthen equality law.

1. It will introduce a new public sector duty to consider the reduction of socio-economic inequalities.

2. It will put a new Equality Duty on public bodies.

3. It will use public procurement to improve equality.

4. It will ban age discrimination outside the workplace.

5. It will introduce gender pay and equality reports.

6. It will extend the scope to use positive action.

7. It will strengthen the powers of employment tribunals.

8. It will protect carers from discrimination.

9. It will protect breastfeeding mothers.

10. It will ban discrimination in private members' clubs.

11. It will strengthen protection from discrimination for people with disabilities.

REFLECTIVE TASK

Positive action

One of the controversial aspects of the single Equality Bill is that it provides for positive action to address discrimination. At the moment it is usually illegal in British law to discriminate positively in favour of a group, even for apparently noble reasons. For example, if three equally qualified applicants apply for an Inspector's post, it would be illegal simply to appoint the black female candidate to address concerns that the constabulary's management was dominated by white men. Equally, it would be illegal to appoint the sole male applicant from four equally qualified primary school teachers to address the fact that all current teaching staff are female. There are two exceptions to this.

- *It is legal to treat people with disabilities favourably. For example, many organisations have a policy of guaranteeing job interviews to all applicants with disabilities who meet the shortlisting criteria.*

- *The PSNI recruits 50 per cent of its new entrants from the Catholic community and 50 per cent from the Protestant community. This is discussed in Chapter 6.*

Positive discrimination is legal in some parts of the world, most notably in South Africa. You will look at these issues further in the chapters on disability and religion.

At first thought, what do you think are the advantages and disadvantages of positive, or reverse, discrimination?

The government also outlines how particular groups will benefit from the introduction of the single Equality Bill.

- The Bill will increase *fairness for women* by allowing positive action in the workplace, extending the powers of employment tribunals and bringing in gender pay reports.

- Bringing in equality reports and extending the use of positive action in the workplace will also make life *fairer for people from ethnic minorities.*

- The Bill will improve *fairness for people with disabilities* by protecting carers from discrimination and by placing duties on landlords to ensure shared housing meets the needs of people with disabilities.

- *Fairness for people of different religions or beliefs* will be improved by requiring public bodies to think about the religious and cultural needs of all who use their services.

- The Bill will improve *fairness for older people* by extending employment legislation beyond the workplace and protecting carers from discrimination.

- *Fairness for lesbian, gay and bisexual people* will be improved by an extension of the use of positive action and the requirement on public bodies to think about the needs of all who use their services.

- *Fairness for transsexual people* will be improved by a revision of the definition of gender reassignment and greater protection for those associated with transsexual people, such as their partners.

The EHRC has strongly welcomed the Equality Bill (EHRC, 2009b). It says that it will ensure that society is fairer and more cohesive and that discrimination is addressed. It will, however, argue that the Bill should be strengthened by including an abolition of the mandatory retirement age, a protection against age discrimination for young people and a further streamlining of legislation relating to harassment.

The Equality Bill

Using the links provided at the end of this chapter, read the single Equality Bill, the accompanying notes and the parliamentary briefing.

PRACTICAL TASK *continued*

- *Do you agree that the Bill will increase fairness in society and streamline current legislation?*

- *What impact do you think the Bill might have on policing?*

Criminological and sociological perspectives

Equality and diversity in society

Throughout this book the legal and policy reasons for promoting equality and respecting diversity will be discussed but, as a starting point, it is important to stress that promoting equality is an ethical imperative. As Banks (2004) sets out, the equality principle requires that people who are equal should be treated equally. Age, disability, gender, religion or sexual orientation should not be a factor. Equality means nothing unless it is applied in a particular context and this book will concentrate on two contexts: first, interaction between the police and members of the public; and, second, relationships within the police organisation.

What is diversity?

Diversity relates to the visible and non-visible differences between people. Valuing diversity allows organisational goals to be met and, at its best, it will result in the celebration of difference. Although many organisations, including national police organisations and almost all local constabularies, refer to diversity, it is rarely defined.

Parekh (2000) identifies three different kinds of diversity: subcultural, perspectival and communal.

- *Subcultural diversity* is used to describe members of groups who share a broad common culture but create distinctive ways of life of their own. They seek to pluralise existing culture. An example of this might be gay or lesbian groups, who share most of society's values and do not seek to transform society, but wish to live safely and comfortably within it.

- *Perspectival diversity* refers to members of society who criticise and seek to change central societal principles. Examples of this might include some political groupings, such as environmentalists and religious groups.

- *Communal diversity* is used to refer to self-conscious, organised communities that live by their own beliefs and practices. These include some immigrant groups and gypsy or traveller communities.

Parekh (2000) draws a distinction between a society that is multicultural, in the sense that it simply contains members of more than one culture, and multiculturalist, which welcomes and respects different cultures.

Much of the discussion relating to diversity has focused on race and ethnicity and, in 1998, the Runnymede Trust set up the Commission on the Future of Multi-Ethnic Britain. The Commission was intended to promote ways of challenging disadvantage and discrimination and to analyse the current situation in Britain. The report suggests a way of responding to diversity that is not merely passive and accepting, but that values diversity in line with six guiding principles (CFMEB, 2000).

1. All individuals have equal worth.

2. Britain is both a community of citizens and a community of communities.

3. Equal treatment needs to take account of difference.

4. Society needs to be both cohesive and respectful of diversity.

5. Human rights principles provide values around which society can unite.

6. Racism can have no place in a decent society.

It is also important, at this early stage, to acknowledge that the criminal justice system as a whole has a poor record in valuing diversity by challenging discrimination. Knight et al. (2008) suggest three reasons for this.

- Those who make policy decisions do not often have the true understanding of diversity that comes through examining their own identity.

- The language used can be ambiguous; the language of diversity is positive and inclusive but does not demand action in the same way as some older terms, such as 'anti-oppressive practice'.

- Good diversity practice does require the investment of resources, but this is usually money well spent, as failing to value diversity can have both indirect and direct costs, through staff sickness, increased turnover and loss of tribunal cases.

So, it is important that we value diversity, but this is not always easy to achieve.

Language

One of the most contentious and difficult issues in relation to respecting and working with diversity concerns language. It is clear that some terms are insulting and offensive and should not be used, particularly by people in positions of responsibility, such as police officers. However, in many other instances, the situation is not nearly so clear-cut. Language can change over time, and terminology that was once commonplace can now be considered offensive. The British Council (2009) provides one example, linked to race:

> *For example, there was a time when 'coloured' was considered polite and 'black' offensive. Nowadays it is precisely the other way round. 'Black' is entirely acceptable and is the preferred term for most people of African or Caribbean heritage. 'Coloured', however, is now no longer acceptable in any context.*

There are many other examples of such changes, including some in the field of disability, such as the use of the word 'spastic', which achieved such negative connotations that the

Spastic Society changed its name to Scope. Conversely, some words that were once offensive have been appropriated by the groups they were once used to describe. It can be confusing and anxiety-provoking to try to navigate the language constraints and to try to find ways to discuss the issues without causing inadvertent offence. The Judicial Studies Board (JSB, 2008) provides some very helpful general guidance, which can also be applied to the police.

- Confidence in the criminal justice system is increased by the considered and thoughtful use of language.

- People who are members of communities that have been subjected to disadvantage are likely to be more sensitive to the language used, and the likely sensitivities connected with the proper use of language cannot be overestimated.

- People involved in the criminal justice system have a right to expect that terminology will be used properly.

- How language is used is a very strong indicator of the attitude of the speaker, and using the right terminology is likely to engender respect.

- It is important that people should always be referred to as people, for example by using terms such as 'people with disabilities' instead of the offensive and dehumanising term 'the disabled'.

REFLECTIVE TASK

Language

Issues of language will be discussed in some individual chapters in this book but, at this stage, think about your own questions and concerns.

- *Is there one aspect of language, or perhaps even an individual term, that you are unsure about?*

- *What might be a good way to determine whether it is generally considered acceptable or offensive?*

Value judgements and ethical frameworks

The notions of equality and diversity are bound up with the question of ethics and decision-making. Police officers are constantly being asked to make decisions about how to act and how to respond to situations. Some of these decisions have a more obvious ethical component than others, but any role-related decision that a police officer on duty makes has an ethical element. For example, a police officer, Adam, who responds to a report of a domestic violence incident to hear the complainant state that there is now no problem when he arrives at the house, has a decision to make that has a strong ethical element. Another police officer, Beena, who responds to a burglary call and notices as she is leaving that the victim's car has no tax disc, also has a decision to make, but this one seems to be much less emotionally and ethically charged. However, the actions of both police officers will have a considerable impact on how the individuals involved view the police.

REFLECTIVE TASK

Value judgements

Before you read the ethical frameworks below, what is your immediate reaction as to how you would respond to the two situations described above? How much freedom does a police officer have to make those decisions?

There are three well-known frameworks that can assist in the making of ethical decisions, and each will be outlined briefly.

The Golden Rule

The Golden Rule is sometimes referred to as the 'rule of reciprocity' and dates back to the teachings of Confucius, Aristotle and Jesus. It can be succinctly stated as:

What you do not want done to yourself, do not do to others.

The rule asks us to treat others as we would wish to be treated in a similar situation. It is often stated as a clear guide to ethical decision-making, but it is probably more realistic to give it the status of a useful principle to consider. One limitation of the Golden Rule is that it is not of sufficient use in situations where there are multiple, and conflicting, viewpoints to take into account. It is clearly not appropriate for a police officer simply to apply the Golden Rule every time he or she encounters a suspected offender, or the police would never carry out any arrests. In Beena's case (above) the Golden Rule would indicate that she should ignore the missing tax disc, as that is what the complainant would want her to do, but would that be correct or ethical? People do not enjoy paying tax, but are still required to do so. In Adam's case, the Golden Rule provides even less help, as it is not even clear exactly what the complainant's wishes are, even before the needs of others are taken into account.

Hooker (2005) suggests that, despite its limitations, the Golden Rule is useful in that, first, it reminds us of moral rules to which we are already committed and, second, it aids the development of our empathy to imagine how our actions might impact on others.

Kantian respect for the individual

Two aspects of the teachings of the philosopher, Immanuel Kant, have taken on the status of general ethical principles. The first of these is the idea that every person should be treated as a self-determining being and be worthy of respect as an individual. We should treat everyone with respect regardless of our own view of them and how they have behaved towards us or other people in the past. This can be a difficult principle for police officers to observe as, by the very nature of their work, they will meet many people who have committed serious and distressing offences. The advice of Bryant et al. (2006) is in line with this principle. They suggest that part of being a professional police officer is the requirement to treat suspects with respect and courtesy even when the offences allegedly committed are as distressing as paedophilia, rape or domestic abuse.

The second Kantian principle is known as the 'categorical imperative', which means that we have an absolute duty to do the right thing and comply with ethical rules at all times. This is a rigid and inflexible approach and leads to implications for police officers, such as in undercover work, which might be considered unethical because of the need for deceit. The ethics of plea bargaining and using informers might also be questioned in such a strict approach as they both involve compromises in the position that similar cases should be dealt with in a similar way.

If Beena took a strictly Kantian approach, she would prosecute the complainant for non-payment of tax. Adam's position is more complicated and demonstrates one of the limitations of Kantian imperatives – that they are of little help when ethical principles conflict with each other. On the one hand, an offence has, allegedly, been committed and this should be properly investigated. On the other hand, the complainant should be treated as a self-determining individual and her wishes should be respected, even though they are in conflict with the wishes expressed shortly before.

Consequentialism/utilitarianism

The third ethical framework is that of consequentialism, or utilitarianism – that the ethics of an action can best be determined by the consequences produced, and an ethical action is one that produces the greatest good for the greatest number of people. The essence of consequentialism is that the end can justify the means. The danger of taking this approach to policing is that it can lead to excesses, such as the use of illegal wire-taps, forced confessions or even torture to achieve the greater ends of peace and security. (Whether such approaches do even lead to greater security is a moot point, but is separate from the ethical discussion.) However, a more moderate approach to consequentialism, expressed as 'acts to produce the best outcomes', would prohibit such excesses (Mason, 2009). A more problematic difficulty with a consequentialist approach is that consequences can be difficult to predict and short-term consequences might differ from long-term consequences. So our hypothetical police officer, Adam, may decide to accept the complainant's request that her original complaint be ignored, fearing that the consequence of an investigation might lead to her suffering further violence. However, the long-term consequences of a failure to act may be even worse. Similarly, his colleague, Beena, may choose to ignore the unpaid car tax, seeking the cooperation of the complainant into the investigation of the much more serious offence of burglary. However, utilitarianism emphasises the need to pay taxes, and being seen to ignore unpaid tax might suggest that the police have a selective approach to tax payment and to the enforcement of the law.

REFLECTIVE TASK

The use of ethical frameworks

Think again about the dilemmas facing Adam and Beena as outlined on page 18.

- *Has a brief consideration of the ethical frameworks helped you to determine what is the right thing to do?*

- *Is this the same as or different from your original reaction?*

- *Do you think any of the frameworks are helpful, either to these dilemmas or to other situations that a police officer might face?*

Equality

As well as promoting diversity, it is also important to give consideration to the concept of equality. Clearly, it is not enough simply to accept that there are many different groups in society; we need to commit to the idea that they are all entitled to equal treatment. The legislation outlined in this chapter and throughout the book aims to achieve this.

There is a variety of reasons why it is right to treat people equally, not least the moral precept that it is the right thing to do, and discrimination should be avoided. However, Wilkinson and Pickett (2009) argue that promoting equality in society is also important in providing benefit for that society. They argue that unequal societies harm everyone, both rich and poor, and that the damage is created in all aspects of society: education, health, employment and criminal justice. They argue that fluctuations in the homicide rate in the USA are closely linked to fluctuations in the measures of equality in that society. More unequal societies are also more inclined to introduce a harsh criminal justice regime and to spend money on prisons and police, rather than welfare and education. The authors' argument is that, if societies wish to reduce their crime rates, it is better for them to take steps towards promoting economic equality than to invest heavily in criminal justice responses such as police and probation services.

Decency

The language of diversity and equality is now established in the police, but it is not the only language used to discuss these issues. The Prison Service uses the language of decency to describe its values. The website states:

> *The Prison Service is dedicated to treating prisoners with decency in a caring and secure environment. This is a very important area of our work and requires [that] our staff develop positive relationships with prisoners. We believe that by treating people with decency, they will be more likely to go on to live useful and law-abiding lives that will benefit them as individuals and society as a whole.*

> *We are committed to ensuring that staff, prisoners and all those visiting prisons or having dealings with the Prison Service are treated fairly and lawfully irrespective of their race, colour, religion, sex or sexual orientation.*
>
> (Prison Service, 2009, no pagination)

As Bennett (2008) outlines, an overarching test for decency, as set out by Phil Wheatley, the Director General of the Prison Service, is whether or not the staff would be happy for a relative of theirs to be housed in a prison. What is particularly distinctive about decency as a values base is that it is measurable. The Prison Service uses a tool called Measuring the Quality of Prison Life (MQPL) to measure prisoners' experiences, covering relationship dimensions (respect, humanity, relationships, trust, support) and regime dimensions (fairness, order, well-being, safety, personal development, family contact) to assess prison performance.

REFLECTIVE TASK

Equality

- *Wilkinson and Pickett, in writing about equality, are mainly referring to economic inequality. How is that relevant to policing? A police officer has little or no power to affect someone's economic status, but why might it be useful to think about these issues?*

- *Is the decency test relevant to policing? Might it be helpful to think about whether you would be happy for a relative of yours to be treated in the way that the police treat an offender or a victim?*

Historical and current police practice

Police culture

All organisations have their own cultures, but police culture perhaps receives more attention than that of other agencies. Organisational culture is the assumptions and beliefs that members of an organisation have about the organisation and its purpose, mission and values. Members of an organisation are rarely able to identify its culture as so much of it relates to unspoken conventions or taken-for-granted assumptions. Organisational culture is particularly important to consider in discussing diversity, as very few organisations will state publically that they wish to discriminate, but some will do so in their informal, day-to-day business (Foster, 2003).

It is tempting to be simplistic in portraying police culture and to describe it as if there is only one dominant culture, with little variation. Foster (2003) quotes American research (Mastrofski et al., 2002), which suggests that there are four main styles that can be attributed to police officers.

- *Professionals* demonstrate knowledge and awareness and good skills of communication and maintaining order.

- *Reactors* are selective about who they help and are reactive, not proactive.

- *Tough cops* take a cynical view and see themselves primarily as crime fighters.

- *Avoiders* would not willingly engage in any encounter.

The professional police officer is what is desired by both the public and the police management, but such officers are still in the minority, although Foster (2003) argues that the different traditions mean that they are more likely to be found in Britain than in the USA.

It is in relation to diversity and difference that the particular nature of police culture becomes apparent:

> *Despite changes in policy [and] recruitment, the police service remains a largely male, white and heterosexual organisation, where those who are perceived to be different by virtue of their race, gender or sexuality have reported significant problems in gaining acceptance and in some cases recognition or legitimacy for their experiences.*
>
> (Foster, 2003, p213)

- Women have often been invisible in police organisations and the dominant ethos is a male, macho one. More sensitive, conciliatory female skills are seen as soft and are not valued.

- Black and minority ethnic officers can find themselves subject to racist language and behaviour, although recently this has become less apparent and more subtle. The police organisation has always been slow to deal with such racism.

- Gay police officers have risked ostracism and lesbian officers can face double discrimination for being both gay and female.

Although Foster paints a fairly depressing picture of police culture, she does suggest that it can be changed, provided the climate is right and the need for change is acknowledged. It is also crucial that police leaders acknowledge the need for change and adopt effective strategies to carry it out.

REFLECTIVE TASK

Police culture

Foster was writing in 2003 and the bullet points, above, reflect her impression of police culture at that time.

- *Do you recognise that picture? Is it an accurate description of the modern police?*

- *If the culture has changed, what do you think has effected that change?*

Although police culture is regularly criticised by those who seek improvement in police performance related to equality and diversity, a more rounded analysis is provided by Waddington (1999). He argues that no real link has been established between police words or actions when among colleagues and any subsequent behaviour, and that researchers should be trying to understand such words and actions rather than simply condemning them. He sees that the necessary task of the police to draw distinctions between 'criminals' and 'citizens' can easily tip over into racism or other forms of bigotry in diverse societies. This is not to justify such attitudes, words or conduct, but simply to put them into the context of the difficult place that the police occupy in society.

Police discretion

One of the reasons why notions of equality and diversity are so important in policing is due to the issue of police discretion. Stenning (2009) provides the *Concise Oxford Dictionary* definition of discretion as the starting point for discussion – 'liberty of deciding as one thinks fit, absolutely or within limits' – and points out that most legislation states that the police 'may' rather than 'shall' take a particular course of action, leaving considerable room for decisions to be made by the police practitioner at the scene. Bryant et al. (2006, p110) give three reasons why it is important that police officers have this discretion and are not simply robots who are programmed to respond to every offence with an arrest, no matter how serious or what the circumstances were.

1. It is not practically feasible.

2. It is not fair.

3. It is not effective.

Discretion relates not just to the decision whether or not to respond to an offence, but also *how* to respond, and what powers to use. It relates both to operational decisions made by police constables and to policy and resource decisions made by more senior managers.

REFLECTIVE TASK

Common sense

A common response from students (not just police students) to being told that they are to be taught about diversity is to say that there is no need for this as it is all just a matter of common sense. Police discretion is sometimes narrowed down to a discussion of common sense, as if all decisions were simple and obvious. It is hoped that, by working through this book, you will appreciate that what is required is a more reflective, sophisticated and informed approach, rather than simply relying on common sense.

This topic is discussed as part of social construction in the chapter on disability, and you will carry out an exercise then to help you reflect on what is meant by 'common sense'. At this stage, try to think of the last time you either heard someone else use the phrase 'common sense' or used it yourself. What was the context, and what was the point that was being made?

The use of discretion by the police has caused some concerns. First, there is a concern about justice. If police officers use discretion, does that mean that one individual might be punished for a particular offence, while another individual might face no sanction for an identical offence? Second, there is a concern about discrimination. As will be discussed throughout this book, many of the concerns that have been expressed about possible discrimination in police practice relate to how discretion is exercised. Some of the criticisms that have been levelled include the following.

- *Race and religion*: the discretionary use of stop-and-search powers has impacted particularly on black people and people perceived to be Muslims.

- *Age*: young people are treated as acting suspiciously, when they are actually behaving in a way that would not be challenged if they were adults.

- *Disability*: the police have been slow to take seriously the concept of disability hate crime.

- *Gender*: offences such as rape and domestic violence have unacceptably low rates of arrest and conviction.

- *Sexuality*: behaviour that would be tolerated in heterosexual couples is treated as suspicious or criminal when engaged in by gay men.

In response to these concerns, there have been steps taken to reduce and structure the scope for police discretion. McLaughlin (2005) summarises these.

- Officers undertake training programmes to enable them to exercise discretion more professionally.

- Ethical principles and guidelines govern the whole organisation.

- Particularly contentious issues related to the use of discretion, such as domestic violence, racial violence, stop and search and the use of deadly force are now covered by internal circulars and codes of practice.

- Strategies are in place to make officers' work practices more visible.

- Internal and external review bodies have been established.

This approach, however, runs the risk of moving too far in the other direction. If police officers are expected to behave in strict accordance with rules and protocols, set down centrally, this can lead to operational difficulties and a deprofessionalisation of the role of the police officer. In particular, it could lead to an unproductive focus on the policing of minor offences, enabling fewer than the required resources to be devoted to more serious offences.

REFLECTIVE TASK

Ethics and discretion

Simon and Burns (2009), in a discussion of the policing of drug use in Baltimore, USA, describe how brown paper bags were used during prohibition (the time in the USA when alcohol was illegal). Police officers were spending so much of their time arresting people drinking on the street that they were unable to devote enough resources to investigating more serious offences. This situation only changed when the street drinkers started holding their bottles in brown paper bags. The police, who previously had no option but to arrest drinkers, could now use their discretion to make the assumption that the liquid in the bottle hidden in the bag was non-alcoholic, and so could ignore these incidents and concentrate resources elsewhere.

- *Do you think this brown paper bag approach was a sensible one?*

- *Look again at the ethical frameworks described on pages 16–18; do you think the approach was ethical?*

Best current police practice and plans for the future

Diversity and the police

In 2003, HMIC (2003, pp62–3) identified that the focus on diversity should not simply relate to race and ethnicity, but should encompass:

- lesbian, gay or bisexual people;

- the deaf or hard of hearing;

- people with mental illness;

- gypsies/travellers;

- people with disabilities;

- victims of domestic violence;

- asylum seekers;

- young people;

- older people;

- transgender people;

- those involved in child protection issues;

- people from areas of poverty (the socially excluded).

Generally, the introduction and organisation of discrimination legislation has led to this list being narrowed down to the six strands of diversity that provide the structure of this book:

- age;

- disability;

- gender;

- race;

- religion;

- sexual orientation.

These are generally accepted to be the strands against which diversity policy should be judged and they appear both in national police guidance and in local policies. Nationally, it is useful to consider what the Integrated Competency Framework (ICF) says about respecting diversity. According to Bryant et al. (2006, p145), police officers are expected to:

- be respectful of the opinions and feelings of all colleagues and members of the public, regardless of their race, religion or other background or characteristics;

- understand and take into account other people's views;

- treat people with dignity, respect, tact and diplomacy;

- show understanding of and sensitivity to social, cultural and racial differences.

As an example of local policies, the Leicestershire Constabulary Equality Scheme (2006) refers to the template that it created to monitor progress against these six strands, and the impact of particular policies and practices. The Chief Executive is required to report annually on progress against this equality scheme. The 2009 report (Leicestershire Police Authority, 2009) stated that action plans were in place in relation to race, sexual orientation, gender and disability, and that action plans were being devised in relation to religion and age. The report provided examples of good practice, such as changes in approach arising from consultation with the Leicestershire Lesbian, Gay, Bisexual and Transgender Forum.

REFLECTIVE TASK

Diversity policy

Find a copy of the diversity policy of your local police constabulary. For most constabularies this should be easily available on the internet, but if it is not you may wish to consider why that is the case, and instead find a policy from a neighbouring force. Read through the policy.

- *Is it clear? Do you know what sort of service to expect from your local police?*

- *Is there anything there that you think should not be there?*

- *Is there anything missing that you would like to see there?*

As discussed throughout this book, the approach of the police to diversity in the early twenty-first century is not merely to respond to an agenda set by others, but to lead society in best diversity practice. Two prominent examples of this are the employment practices of those police constabularies who have been nominated as gay-friendly employers by Stonewall (see Chapter 7); and the PSNI, which is leading integration in Northern Ireland by addressing the long-standing under-representation of Catholics in the police force.

Hate crime

Throughout this book it will become clear that one of the most challenging aspects for the police in working in a modern, diverse society is in responding to hate crime. Although crimes inspired by hatred of individuals or groups are not new, the concept of 'hate crime' is a relatively recent addition to the language of offending in the UK. The term does have a longer history in the USA. High-profile incidents, such as the murder of Stephen Lawrence, the Admiral Duncan bombings and the increase in tensions with the Muslim community following the 9/11 and July 2007 terrorist attacks, have all led to a higher profile for hate crime (Chakraborti and Garland, 2009). However, despite the increasing prominence of the term, there is no one settled definition of hate crime, nor is there a consensus as to what it is. Academic definitions emphasise that the perpetrator does not actually need to hate the victim; hate crime is often established simply through an acknowledgement that the victim belongs to a particular group. Hate crimes must be understood within a societal context.

For police purposes, in the UK, the main official definition of hate crime can be found in guidance from the Association of Chief Police Officers (ACPO, 2000, 2005). The 2005 guidelines provide a definition of a hate incident and of a hate crime:

A hate incident is defined as:

> *Any incident, which may or may not constitute a criminal offence, which is perceived by the victim or any other person as being motivated by prejudice or hate.*

A hate crime is defined as:

> *Any hate incident, which constitutes a criminal offence, perceived by the victim or any other person as being motivated by prejudice or hate.*

As Chakraborti and Garland (2009) highlight in their discussion of these definitions, the presence of hatred is not actually required – the presence of prejudice is sufficient. This prejudice should be against particular groups, identified by ACPO as prejudice on the basis of race, sexual orientation, faith or disability. The relevant legislation reflects this; although there is no single hate crime law, there are a number of recent statutes that together provide the legal framework for hate crime (Chakraborti and Garland, 2009).

- Sections 28–32 of the Crime and Disorder Act 1998 introduced enhanced penalties related to racially aggravated offences, so that offenders guilty of such offences could receive more severe sentences.

- The Anti-Terrorism, Crime and Security Act 2001 extends this principle to religiously aggravated offences.

- Section 146 of the Criminal Justice Act 2003 gives courts the power to impose heavier sentences when crimes are motivated by the victim's sexuality or mental or physical disability.

- Laws prohibiting incitement are contained in the Public Order Act 1986, the Racial and Religious Hatred Act 2006 and the Criminal Justice and Immigration Act 2008.

The introduction of specific legislation on hate crime has not been welcomed by all commentators, and Newburn (2007) identifies three possible problems with hate crime legislation.

- The legislation is framed in such a way that it might lead to minor crimes being targeted, while leaving much more serious forms of racism untouched.

- The legislation could lead to similar victims being treated in different ways. For example, a victim of an offence that is not defined as being motivated by hatred might feel that he or she has been treated unfairly compared to a victim of a hate crime. This could increase and exaggerate differences between groups.

- The police may simply use the legislation as a way of adding additional punishment to selected offenders, without necessarily targeting those with a particularly racist motivation.

REFLECTIVE TASK

Proving hate crime

Hate crime against specific groups will be considered in the relevant chapters throughout this book. One of the difficulties in gaining convictions for offences of hate crime is an evidential one – it is hard to prove that an offender is motivated by hate, or even by prejudice. Can you think of any ways in which it might be possible to prove such an offence?

C H A P T E R   S U M M A R Y

This chapter has provided an introduction to the main issues relating to diversity and policing. The legislative and policy context has been covered in detail, so you will be aware both of the present situation and of the changes that are planned for the future. This chapter has also covered ethical frameworks to provide you with a framework for making the difficult decisions that are a familiar part of all criminal justice work, and to help you to understand some of the history in thinking about ethics that exists in all parts of the criminal justice system. It is hoped that, through reading this chapter, you will recognise that there is both an ethical and a legal case for promoting human rights and diversity in policing and that it is vital for effective police practice. Throughout the book, the two main themes of promoting diversity within the organisation and of engaging in best equality and diversity practice in dealing with the public will remain prominent.

This book will now follow the structure of the six strands of diversity with each of the following six chapters concentrating on one of those strands and its relationship to police practice. It will be worthwhile to keep in mind the material in this chapter – particularly about the legislative context, human rights and the ethical frameworks – while working through the rest of the book. It is also important to remember that the promotion of human rights and the habit of best diversity practice are not skills to be turned on and off when members of the six particular groups are encountered; they should be embedded in every aspect of work of a police officer.

REFERENCES

Association of Chief Police Officers (ACPO) (2000) *Guide to Identifying and Combating Hate Crime*. London: ACPO.

Association of Chief Police Officers (ACPO) (2005) *Hate Crime: Delivering a Quality Service – Good Practice and Tactical Guidance*. London: Home Office Police Standards Unit.

Banks, C (2004) *Criminal Justice Ethics*. Thousand Oaks, CA: Sage.

Bennett, J (2008) Decency, in Jewkes, Y and Bennett, J (eds) *Dictionary of Prisons and Punishment*. Cullompton: Willan.

Bingham, T (2009) Key note address at Liberty's 75th Anniversary Conference. Available online at www.liberty-human-rights.org.uk/about/1-history/75th-anniversary-conference/key-note-address-by-lord-bingham-at-liberty-s-75th-anniversary-conference.pdf (accessed 15 August 2009).

British Council (2009) Equal Opportunity at the British Council. Available online at www.britishcouncil. org/home-diversity.htm (accessed 10 March 2010).

Bryant, R, Caless, B, Lawton-Barrett, K, Underwood, R and Wood, D (2006) *Blackstone's Student Police Officer Handbook*. Oxford: Oxford University Press.

Chakraborti, N and Garland, J (2009) *Hate Crime: Impact, Causes and Responses*, London: Sage.

Commission on the Future of Multi-Ethnic Britain (CFMEB) (2000) *The Future of Multi-Ethnic Britain: The Parekh Report*. London: Profile Books for the Runnymede Trust.

Equality and Human Rights Commission (EHRC) (2009a) *Human Rights Enquiry*. Available online at www.equalityhumanrights.com/human-rights/human-rights-inquiry/inquiry-report/ (accessed 15 August 2009).

Equality and Human Rights Commission (EHRC) (2009b) *Equality Bill – Parliamentary Briefing*. Available online at www.equalityhumanrights.com/uploaded_files/equality_bill_parl_brief_0509.pdf (accessed 15 August 2009).

Foster, J (2003) Police cultures, in Newburn, T (ed.) *Handbook of Policing*. Cullompton: Willan.

Her Majesty's Inspectorate of Constabulary (HMIC) (2003) *Diversity Matters*. London: The Home Office.

Her Majesty's Inspectorate of Constabulary (HMIC) (2009) *Adapting to Protest*. London: HMIC. Available online at http://news.bbc.co.uk/1/shared/bsp/hi/pdfs/07_07_09_g20_police_report.pdf (accessed 10 March 2010).

Hooker, B (2005) The Golden Rule. *Think*, 10: 25–9.

Judicial Studies Board (JSB) (2008) *Equal Treatment Bench Book: 1.1 Equality and Justice*. Available online at www.jsboard.co.uk/etac/downloads/equality_and_justice.doc (accessed 10 March 2010).

Knight, C, Dominey, J and Hudson, J (2008) 'Diversity': contested meanings and differential consequences, in Stout, B, Yates, J and Williams, B (eds) *Applied Criminology*. London: Sage.

Laville, S (2009) New ACPO Chief wants human rights to be put at core of policing. *The Guardian*, 21 June. Available online at www.guardian.co.uk/politics/2009/jun/21/hugh-orde-acpo-human-rights (accessed 15 August 2009).

Leicestershire Constabulary (2006) *Leicestershire Constabulary Equality Scheme 2006–2008*. Available online at www.leics.police.uk/files/library/documents/LC-Equality-Scheme-Dec-2006-2008-Updated-Nov-07b.pdf (accessed 15 August 2009).

Leicestershire Police Authority (2009) *Police Authority Equality Scheme Update*. Available online at www.leics-pa.police.uk/files/library/paper-g-pa-equality-scheme.pdf (accessed 15 August 2009).

Lyon, J (2009) *Why Prisoners Need the Vote*. Available online at www.prisonreformtrust.org.uk/standard.asp?id=1733 (accessed 15 August 2009).

Mason, E (2009) What is consequentialism? *Think*, 8: 19–28.

Mastrofski, S, Willis, J and Snipes, J (2002) Styles of patrol in a community policing context, in Morash, M and Ford, J (eds) *The Move to Community Policing*. Thousand Oaks, CA: Sage, pp81–111.

McLaughlin, E (2005) Discretion, in McLaughlin, E And Muncie, J (eds) *The Sage Dictionary of Criminology*. London: Sage.

Ministry of Justice (2009) *Prisoner Voting: Second Stage Consultation*. Available online at www.justice.gov.uk/news/newsrelease080409b.htm (accessed 15 August 2009).

Mulcahy, A (2006) *Policing Northern Ireland: Conflict, Legitimacy and Reform*. Cullompton: Willan.

Murphy, K (2009) Legitimacy, in Wakefield, A and Fleming, J (eds) *The Sage Dictionary of Policing*. London: Sage.

Newburn, T (2003) Policing since 1945, in Newburn, T (ed.) *Handbook of Policing*. Cullompton: Willan.

Newburn, T (2007) *Criminology*. Cullompton: Willan.

O'Loan, N (2009) My lessons for the Police, *The Guardian*, 26 June. Available online at www.guardian.co.uk/commentisfree/2009/jun/26/human-rights-police-northern-ireland (accessed 15 August 2009)

Parekh, B (2000) *Rethinking Multiculturalism – Cultural Diversity and Political Theory*. Basingstoke: Palgrave.

Prison Service (2009) *Decency*. Available online at www.hmprisonservice.gov.uk/abouttheservice/decency/ (accessed 10 March 2010).

Rowe, M (2008) *Introduction to Policing*. London: Sage.

Scraton, P (2009) *Hillsborough: The Truth*. Edinburgh and London: Mainstream Publishing.

Simon, D and Burns, E (2009) *The Corner*. Canongate: Edinburgh.

Stenning, P (2009) Discretion, in Wakefield, A and Fleming, J (eds) *The Sage Dictionary of Policing*. London: Sage.

Straw, J (2009) Changing the face of human rights, speech delivered to the annual conference of the British Institute of Human Rights, 28 January. Available online at www.justice.gov.uk/news/sp280109.htm (accessed 15 August 2009).

Waddington, P A J (1999) Police (canteen) sub-culture: an appreciation. *British Journal of Criminology*, 39(2): 287–309.

Wilkinson, R and Pickett, K (2009) *The Spirit Level: Why Equal Societies Almost Always Do Better*. London: Allen Lane.

<table>
<tr><td>

FURTHER READING

</td><td>

Much of the reading related to this book is connected to particular strands of diversity, so it will be recommended in the relevant chapters. However, there are two websites that you will be asked to refer to regularly and you should familiarise yourself with them at this stage.

</td></tr>
</table>

The first of these is the website of the Equality and Human Rights Commission (www.equalityhumanrights.com/), which contains legislation, policy, guidance and campaigning information on all aspects of diversity and equality. It is not compulsory for you to agree with everything produced by the Commission, but you should certainly be familiar with the key material produced.

The second website is that of your own local police constabulary. Its website is one of the main ways in which a police force can communicate with the community it serves, and it can be very revealing as to what its priorities are. It is useful to know both what it says about each strand of diversity, and how easily this information can be accessed.

If you are a police student, you are probably already familiar with *Blackstone's Student Police Officer Handbook* (Bryant et al., 2006) and the material in this book should complement that essential text. Tim Newburn's *Criminology* (2007) is the key criminological introductory text and much of the material on criminological theory in each chapter of this book has been sourced from there. Hate crime is a relatively recent area of study and Neil Chakraborti and Jon Garland's (2009) text, *Hate Crime*, has been used throughout this book to provide the most up-to-date material on this topic. It is highly recommended if you wish to learn more about hate crime.

This book is part of a Learning Matters series and should be read in conjunction with the other books in the series (see the Learning Matters website at www.learningmatters.co.uk for details of these). Equality and diversity are not just subjects in their own right, but influence and inform all aspects of police policy and practice.

USEFUL WEBSITES

All weblinks and web addresses in the book have been carefully checked prior to publication, but for up-to-date information please visit the Learning Matters website at www.learningmatters.co.uk.

www.britishcouncil.org/home-diversity.htm (British Council)

www.coe.int/ (Council of Europe)

www.echr.coe.int/ECHR/homepage_en (European Court of Human Rights)

www.equalities.gov.uk/Default.aspx (Government Equalities Office)

www.equalityhumanrights.com/ (Equality and Human Rights Commission)

www.hmprisonservice.gov.uk/ (Prison Service)

www.justice.gov.uk/index.htm (Ministry of Justice)

www.liberty-human-rights.org.uk/ (Liberty)

www.prisonreformtrust.org.uk/index.asp?id=1 (Prison Reform Trust)

www.skillsforjustice-nosfinder.com (National Occupational Standards)

2 Age

Introduction

Age discrimination legislation mainly relates to employment provisions and the need to protect the rights of an ageing workforce (Bryant et al., 2006), so initially it appears that there is little relevance to police practice. Employment legislation is considered as part of this chapter, and attention is also given to elder abuse and the question of whether it can be considered to be a hate crime. However, there is a lot to be discussed about the relationship between the police and children and young people. This chapter will mainly concern itself with how young people are responded to by the criminal justice system in general, and specifically by the police. After an introduction to the relevant policy and legislation, there will be a discussion of the consideration given to young people by the criminal justice system, including a historical and international perspective. Some of the ways in which the criminal justice system has responded to young people will then be discussed, and the final section will outline the different ways in which police officers and Police Community Support Officers (PCSOs) now work with young people.

Policy and legislation

The legislation outlawing discrimination on the basis of age is contained in the Employment Equality (Age) Regulations 2006. These protect against age discrimination in all aspects of employment. The government's website (Directgov, 2009) provides examples of this protection.

- *Redundancy protection*: any redundancy policies must not unduly impact on young or old workers.

- *Retirement rights*: retirement at 65 is not compulsory and an employer will have to give reasons for retiring someone at an earlier age.

- *Unfair dismissal*: there is no upper age limit on making a claim.

- *Training*: upper or lower age limits should not normally be set.

- *Service-related benefits*: if employment benefits are connected to length of service, that service must not be for more than five years.

Age-related discrimination is only permitted when it can be objectively justified, such as for health and safety reasons.

PRACTICAL TASK

Could you police?

The 'Police: Could You?' website (2009) provides guidance for those who wish to join the police and it states, with regard to age requirements:

> *Applications can be accepted at the age of 18. There's no upper age limit for applying to the police service, but bear in mind that the normal retirement age is 60 years and that new recruits are required to undertake a two-year probationary period.*

Police recruitment includes fitness, health and eyesight tests and suitability is determined on the basis of these tests, rather than on assumptions about what people of a particular age can or cannot do.

What do you think the objective justification might be for making the normal retirement age 60, rather than 65?

The key legislation relating to the control of young people's behaviour will be referred to in the main body of the chapter. However, at this stage it is important to highlight the Criminal Justice and Immigration Act 2008, which deals with the sentencing of convicted young offenders. This abolished existing orders and replaced them with one youth rehabilitation order. There is now just one community sentence, with a list of requirements that can be added, which can include activities, exclusions, drug testing and measures for very serious offenders, including intensive supervision and surveillance, and intensive fostering (Muncie, 2009).

Criminological and sociological perspectives

As will be discussed later in the chapter, there has been considerable concern about crime committed by children and young people in the last decade, and this has led the government to respond with a variety of measures and interventions. It would be easy to believe that society is in decline and that the behaviour of young people is much worse than it used to be. However, a study of the history of youth justice makes it clear that youth crime has been a subject of concern for some time. For example, Muncie (2009) provides a list of quotations from the past to illustrate his point that concern about youth behaviour is nothing new. One of these quotations, which has a contemporary feel, is:

> *The manners of children are deteriorating . . . the child of today is coarser, more vulgar, less refined than his parents were.*

That statement was made in 1898.

Although it is tempting to think of childhood and adulthood as biological certainties (a person below a certain age is a child and a person above that age is an adult), it is important to remember that the concepts of childhood and youth are socially constructed (social construction is discussed in detail in the next chapter). It was only in the Middle Ages that childhood and adulthood were considered to be different entities. Children were seen as being both innocent and in need of direction, and this duality still influences responses to young people's behaviour. Until the middle of the nineteenth century, a protected childhood was really a middle-class luxury; children of poorer families were treated as possessions and were required to go out to work (Muncie, 2009).

It was also in the nineteenth century that concerns began to be expressed about juvenile delinquency, but the initial response was to blame neglectful parents for the fact that young people were committing crimes at an earlier age. Children were, however, increasingly being drawn into the criminal justice system and facing a whole range of penalties, including transportation to Australia, often as an alternative to the death penalty. Prison reformers campaigned for the separate imprisonment of children from adults and then for improvement in those prison conditions. This separate regime, combined with an increased police role in detecting youth crime, led to an expansion in the juvenile justice system throughout the following two centuries (Muncie, 2009).

One of the important themes running through the history of the criminal justice system is that of the age of criminal responsibility. From around the middle of the fourteenth century, children under the age of 14 were deemed to be 'doli incapax', or incapable of evil. This only changed in the 1990s, as part of a fundamental shake-up of youth justice legislation and policy following the murder of James Bulger.

James was a two-year-old boy who was abducted and murdered by two ten-year-olds. The public shock at this murder caused the government to respond by reforming youth justice provision along the lines expressed by Prime Minister John Major, who said that 'Society should condemn a little more and understand a little less' (Smith, 2007). Both main political parties argued that the principle of doli incapax should no longer apply and it was eventually abolished by the Crime and Disorder Act 1998. The age of criminal responsibility is now eight in Scotland and ten in England, Wales and Northern Ireland (Muncie, 2009).

Criminal responsibility

The age of criminal responsibility has quite an important effect on police practice with young people. If, say, a 12-year-old is below the age of criminal responsibility, he or she can simply be referred to social services after coming to police attention. However, if the child is criminally responsible, the role of the police, and the rest of the criminal justice system, is much more significant.

- *How do you think the age of criminal responsibility should be determined?*

- *What are the advantages and disadvantages of holding very young children (between the ages of 8 and 12) criminally responsible for their actions?*

- *What particular skills should be possessed by a police officer working with children under the age of 12?*

The age of criminal responsibility is just one of the areas in which national legislation is influenced by international instruments. With regard to criminal responsibility, however, the UK position is notable for being out of step with other European countries and contrary to the recommendations of international instruments:

> *In the European Union these ages range from 8 in Scotland, and 10 in England and Wales, to 15 in Denmark, Norway, Finland and Sweden and 18 in Belgium and Luxembourg.*

> (Muncie and Goldson, 2006, p199)

According to Muncie (2009), the main international instruments that influence youth justice are as follows.

- *The 1985 United Nations Standard Minimum Rules for the Administration of Youth Justice (Beijing Rules)*. These promote diversion and the minimum use of custody.

- *The 1989 United Nations Convention on the Rights of the Child (UNCRC)*. This establishes that all children have the right to protection, participation and basic material provision.

- *The 1990 United Nations Guidelines for the Prevention of Juvenile Delinquency (Riyadh Guidelines)*. These stated that trivial offences and misdemeanours should not lead to the criminalisation of children.

These instruments have less influence on UK policy and practice than they do on some other jurisdictions, but it is worth remembering that youth justice practice does not simply take place in a national framework, but in an international context.

Historical and current police practice

Young people are treated differently from adults by the criminal justice system. As discussed above, the original reason for this differential treatment was that children were considered not to have the full criminal capacity, or ability, to tell right from wrong, as adults do. However, it is now much more the case that criminal justice legislation directly targets young people, either by criminalising behaviour that only young people engage in, or by directing resources to control young people's actions. Police practice is led by such legislation and three examples are considered below: the ASBO, the dispersal order and the mosquito. These are all connected to the government's 'Respect' agenda and affect the interaction between young people and the police, often in the form of PCSOs, whose role in neighbourhood policing puts them at the forefront of the relationship between young people and the criminal justice system.

The ASBO

The anti-social behaviour order (ASBO) was introduced by the Crime and Disorder Act 1998, but was not initially targeted mainly at young people. However, as the government gave greater prominence to responding to concerns about young people's disorder and offending, the ASBO was increasingly used against young people. By 1995, over 40 per cent of ASBOs had been issued against those under the age of 18 (McAra, 2008).

Smith (2007) identifies that the ASBO is particularly likely to lead to discrimination against young people. It concentrates on behaviour likely to be perpetrated by young people and targets those who are particularly high-profile, such as those with Tourette's syndrome or autism. The campaigning group ASBOwatch collects examples of how ASBOs have been used and these include the following (ASBOwatch, 2009).

- A 16-year-old boy banned from entering school grounds, gardens or car parks throughout England and Wales, without an invitation.

- A 16-year-old boy who was given an ASBO forbidding him from meeting with his friends, and who subsequently received a four-month period of detention for breaching this order.

- A 12-year-old boy who was given an evening curfew for at least five years.

- A 14-year-old boy banned from wearing a hooded top with the hood up, except when the weather is bad.

ASBOs are also used to prevent behaviour that is already prohibited (such as drinking alcohol) and councils now have the power to apply for so-called 'baby ASBOs' for children under the age of ten. In an example of how different strands of diversity can overlap, there is an over-representation, at 22 per cent, of black and Asian young people in the population of those receiving an ASBO (Muncie, 2008).

Dispersal orders and curfews

The government built on the response to anti-social behaviour in 2003 with the publication of the paper, *Respect and Responsibility: Taking a Stand against Anti-social Behaviour* (Home Office, 2003), and the subsequent Anti-social Behaviour Act 2003. The language of respect was thus placed at the centre of the response to young people's behaviour. The two provisions of the Act that have the greatest impact on young people are the curfew and the dispersal order.

Curfews can be imposed on individual young people between the ages of 10 and 15 and can either be imposed alongside another order or can act as a stand-alone disposal. A curfew requires the young person to be at a certain place between specified hours, and the order can be imposed for up to six months. The legislative basis for imposing curfews is now contained in the Criminal Justice and Immigration Act 2008, which created the youth rehabilitation order. It is easy to see how a curfew might be of benefit to a serious young offender undergoing rehabilitation in the community, but when they are imposed on their own, they can have little rehabilitative impact (Walsh, 2008). Curfews can also raise the anxiety both of parents and of vulnerable people in the community (Muncie, 2009).

The monitoring of curfews is increasingly being carried out electronically, but there is still a significant police role, which can lead to tension and conflict between young people and the police. Muncie (2009) gives the example of Strathclyde Police imposing a dusk to dawn curfew on all young people under the age of 16 on particular estates. This is legislated for in the Crime and Disorder Act 1998, section 14, and has a similar impact to a dispersal order (Bryant et al., 2006).

Dispersal orders were created by the Anti-social Behaviour Act 2003, which allows the police to disperse people from areas where there is perceived to be a risk of intimidation or other anti-social behaviour. Police superintendents are able, in consultation with local authorities, to declare particular areas as dispersal zones. Over 1,000 areas in England and Wales have been declared dispersal zones (Minton, 2009). Again, the legislation does not limit the use of dispersal orders to young people (and they are used against adult prostitutes and beggars), but they are primarily used against young people. The police have a lot of discretion in the use of dispersal order powers, particularly as young people do not actually have to commit an offence before they are dispersed. It is simply enough for the police to judge that their conduct is likely to cause offence (Crawford, 2008). Minton (2009) is highly critical of how these orders have been used, saying that the effect has been simply to allow the police to approach young people and tell them to go home, even if they are doing nothing more than visiting a fast-food outlet or playing in the street.

REFLECTIVE TASK

Respect

ASBOs, curfews and dispersal orders all form part of the government's 'Respect' agenda. This was introduced as a response to public concern about the behaviour of young people, and the government would say that it has had some success in alleviating that concern. However, critics argue that the policies demonise young people, stretch police resources and create constant tension between the police and the community.

- *What does the word 'respect' mean to you?*

- *What does it mean for a young person to behave respectfully?*

- *What does it mean for a police officer to treat a young person with respect?*

- *Does this change depend on whether the young person is a victim, a member of the public or a known offender?*

The mosquito

The mosquito ultrasonic device is perhaps the clearest example of an intervention being deliberately and explicitly targeted at young people. The device produces a sound that is designed to make the listener feel ill, but it only works on those under the age of 25, who have more sensitive hearing than older people. Muncie (2009) quotes the description provided by the producers:

> *The mosquito ultrasonic teenage deterrent is the solution to the eternal problem of unwanted gatherings of youths and teenagers in shopping malls, around shops and anywhere else they are causing problems. The presence of these teenagers discourages genuine shoppers and customers from coming into your shop, affecting your turnover and profits. Anti-social behaviour has become the biggest threat to private property over the last decade and there has been no effective deterrent until now.*

(2009, p259)

Minton (2009) spoke to a young people's manager in Salford about the effect of the use of the mosquito on the community there. This manager was described as 'incandescent' about such a device being used in her community, where it could cause illness to any child indiscriminately. In this community, the original proposal had been to place the mosquito at a bus-stop, where, as the manager described, it could have caused significant distress to any child, particularly a baby in a pram, who happened to be waiting for a bus. The use of the mosquito was perceived by young people as treating them with disrespect, while requiring them to show respect to others.

REFLECTIVE TASK

The mosquito

Minton quoted the young people's manager she interviewed as saying about the mosquito:

> *It's obviously totally against human rights. Imagine putting something up that pierced the ears of black or disabled people.*

> *(2009, p159)*

Do you think this is a fair comparison? If so, why is it fair, and, if not, why not?

Best current police practice and plans for the future

Age-related hate crime

Although this chapter is focusing on young people, it is important not to ignore the fact that older people can be particularly vulnerable to the effects of offending. There are instances of both the old and the young being targeted by what might be considered age-related hate crime. However, unlike other instances of hate crime discussed in this book, there is no universal acknowledgement from the police, and other commentators, that offences against older people constitute hate crime. Chakraborti and Garland (2009) found that only a third of the police forces in Great Britain considered such offences to be hate crime. Elder abuse can include physical or psychological abuse, as well as neglect. Help the Aged (2009) state that 'Elder abuse occurs when older men or women are harmed, mistreated or neglected.' The organisation gives examples of how this abuse could be perpetrated by a carer.

- *Neglect* can involve failing to provide food or water, or basic washing and cleaning services.
- *Sexual abuse* can range from unwelcome explicit jokes to inappropriate touching.
- *Physical abuse* can include rough handling or deliberate acts of violence.
- *Emotional abuse* is often about gaining power, and can include verbal abuse, criticism or even simply the withholding of affection.
- *Financial abuse* could include a trusted carer taking money or an act of fraud carried out by a conman.

The advice of Help the Aged in all these situations is that, if elderly people suspect that they may be the victims of any of these forms of abuse, they should contact the police. The police are also recommended as a proactive source of advice and support. However, there remains a low level of reporting of such crimes, as it is very difficult to acknowledge that a carer, who might be a family member, could be a source of abuse. Chakraborti and Garland (2009) report that there is also evidence to suggest that older people are not always believed when they report such instances. This is a similar pattern to that which occurs when people with disabilities report hate crime.

REFLECTIVE TASK

Elder abuse

As stated earlier, a third of police forces describe elder abuse as a hate crime. For example, an information leaflet produced by the Essex Criminal Justice Board states:

> Hate crime includes domestic violence, crimes against race, belief, different sects, gay, lesbian, bisexual, transgender, disabled people, **the elderly**, other vulnerable adults or young people.
>
> (2009, p1; my emphasis)

Chakraborti and Garland (2009) suggest that, although elder abuse needs to be taken seriously, and older people are particularly vulnerable to crime and abuse, it is stretching the definition too far to conceptualise all offences against older people as age-related hate crime. They argue that older people, many of whom might be wealthy and holding respected positions in society, cannot be considered to be a disadvantaged group in the same way as some other groups might be.

- Do you think it is accurate and helpful to describe elder abuse as a 'hate crime'?

- What might be gained and what might be lost by describing it in that way?

Working with young people

As we have seen throughout this chapter, it is challenging for the police to develop positive relationships with the young people in a community. These difficulties and tensions cannot simply be linked to instances of police practice, but instead flow directly from the legislative and policy framework. The 'Respect' agenda has placed many restrictions on young people and, as police services are the agencies that are tasked with enforcing this legislation, it is, perhaps, unsurprising that researchers have found that police officers are sometimes viewed negatively by young people.

Smith (2007) found that young people generally held the same morals and values as the wider community, but had a more difficult relationship with the formal criminal justice system. Young people interviewed said that they wanted to be taken seriously when they reported a crime; they wanted to be treated non-judgementally; and they wanted the police to earn their respect rather than assume that it would simply be given. Young black people, in particular, wanted the police to demonstrate more courtesy and take more of an interest in their concerns. Other criminal justice agencies provoked a slightly better reaction, but the overall effect is that there are difficulties with acceptance of the legitimacy of the criminal justice system.

Webster (2006) is extremely critical of the police approach to young black people, particularly in the 1970s and 1980s, and goes on to criticise the police for taking a similar approach to young Asian people in the 1990s. His contention is that police practice has criminalised young black people and caused them to be 'recruited' into the criminal justice system. These issues will be discussed in greater detail in Chapter 5.

It is, however, important not simply to focus on the negative aspects of police practice with young people, as there are also instances of excellent practice in building relationships between the two groups. The most prominent example of this is police-led restorative cautioning. Restorative justice is a different way of dealing with criminal justice than the traditional retributive justice system, in that it emphasises the relationship between the victim and the offender and the need to repair that relationship following the commission of the offence. It has been introduced in different ways in different jurisdictions, but two UK examples are given here of police-led cautioning in Thames Valley and Northern Ireland.

Thames Valley Police is credited with introducing restorative justice to England in 1995, following the example of the Wagga Wagga police district in Australia. The model included input from victims and the families of both offenders and victims, so that, rather than the offender simply being scolded by a police officer, with whom they had no ongoing relationship, he or she would also have to face the victim who had been damaged by the offence, and his or her own closest family. Restorative justice is based on the idea that this 'reintegrative shaming' would have a significant effect on the offender and encourage a change in behaviour, while retaining relationships with those closest to the offender. Research into this scheme (described by Haines and O'Mahoney, 2006) found a high level of victim satisfaction (albeit among a relatively small number of victims who attended), but no significant difference in reoffending rates compared to a traditional cautioning system. However, building on the partial success of this approach, restorative justice was introduced nationally into the youth justice system, through youth offending teams (YOTs), in the Crime and Disorder Act 1998 and in the Youth Justice and Criminal Evidence Act 1999.

Restorative justice is even more central to the Northern Ireland youth justice system and, again, research found that police-led restorative justice schemes were an improvement on previous cautioning practice (Haines and O'Mahoney, 2006), in terms of the responses of both offenders and victims. One of the most significant positive effects to come out of this scheme was the transformation in views of the police and the change in relationships between police and community:

> The research found the police to be enthusiastic and sincerely committed to the restorative process. They had been well trained and it was clear from the interviews with the young people and parents that they placed a high degree of confidence in and support for the scheme. There was also some evidence that it had other beneficial effects especially in terms of helping improve police/community relations, which have been considerably strained over the years of conflict.
>
> (Haines and O'Mahoney, 2006, p115)

Northern Ireland now has a restorative conferencing model, legislatively based in the Justice (Northern Ireland) Act 2002 and led by the Youth Conferencing Service.

Hoyle and Young (2003) make the important point that, as well as changing the relationship between the police and young offenders, restorative justice also brings the police into much closer contact with crime victims and ties their interests together much more closely.

Restorative interventions

As discussed above, there is evidence to suggest that restorative interventions are successful in changing the behaviour of young people. However, restorative cautioning also creates a different relationship between the police, offenders and victims, and requires a very different approach to some other police work, such as, for example, enforcing a dispersal order.

- *Imagine that you are a serving police officer. Which would you feel more comfortable doing: facilitating a restorative conference or enforcing a dispersal order?*

- *Which do you think is a more appropriate police role? Is there a place for both?*

Another situation in which police officers and young people might come into contact is through youth offending teams (YOTs). These were created by the Crime and Disorder Act 1998, and are multi-agency teams including representatives from health, education, social and probation services, as well as the police. The work of YOTs is monitored by the Youth Justice Board (YJB) All staff, including police officers, are expected to work flexibly, in a way that not only reflects their personal and professional background, but also meets the needs and the identity of the YOT. Although some police forces, and other agencies, choose to give money to the local YOT, rather than second staff, there are still many opportunities for police constables to work in YOTs (Thomas, 2008).

C H A P T E R   S U M M A R Y

The police have a very difficult role to play with young people. On the one hand, occasionally a young person will commit a very serious crime and the persistent anti-social behaviour of some groups of young people can cause great anxiety and distress to sections of the community. The political guidance to the police is to deal with this very seriously and to treat young people as potential troublemakers. On the other hand, the vast majority of children and young people are well behaved and law-abiding. They are a vulnerable group, entitled to police protection. In this respect, they are similar to the elderly population. Police forces have the tricky task of enforcing legislation that is proactive and severe in its impact on young people, while also working in a restorative and engaging way in cautioning and in YOTs. Individual officers require a complex set of skills in fulfilling one or more of these roles.

REFERENCES

ASBOwatch (2009) Cases of ASBOs used against children. Available online at www.statewatch.org/asbo/ASBOwatch.html (accessed 10 March 2010).

Bryant, R, Caless, B, Lawton-Barrett, K, Underwood, R and Wood, D (2006) *Blackstone's Student Police Officer Handbook*. Oxford: Oxford University Press.

Chakraborti, N and Garland, J (2009) *Hate Crime: Impact, Causes and Responses*. London: Sage.

Crawford, A. (2008) Dispersal orders, in Goldson, B (ed.) *Dictionary of Youth Justice*. Cullompton: Willan.

Directgov (2009) *Age Discrimination*. Available online at www.direct.gov.uk/en/Employment/ResolvingWorkplaceDisputes/DiscriminationAtWork/DG_10026429 (accessed 10 March 2010).

Essex Criminal Justice Board (2009) *Hate Crime – A Menace in Society*. Available online at http://lcjb.cjsonline.gov.uk/Essex/home.html (accessed 15 August 2009).

Haines, K and O'Mahoney, D (2006) Restorative approaches, young people and youth justice, in Goldson, B (ed.) *Youth Crime and Justice*. London: Sage.

Help the Aged (2009) Frequently asked questions. Available online at www.helptheaged.org.uk/en-gb/AdviceSupport/ (accessed 10 March 2010).

Home Office (2003) *Respect and Responsibility: Taking a Stand against Anti-social Behaviour.* London: Home Office.

Hoyle, C and Young, R (2003) Restorative justice, victims and the police, in Newburn, T (ed.) *Handbook of Policing*. Cullompton: Willan.

McAra, L (2008) 'Anti-social behaviour orders (ASBOs), in Goldson, B (ed.) *Dictionary of Youth Justice*. Cullompton: Willan.

Minton, A (2009) *Ground Control: Fear and Happiness in the Twenty-first Century*. London: Penguin.

Muncie, J (2009) *Youth and Crime*, – 3rd edition. London: Sage.

Muncie, J and Goldson, B (2006) 'States of transition: convergence and diversity in international youth justice, in Muncie, J and Goldson, B (eds) *Comparative Youth Justice*. London: Sage.

Police: Could You? (2009) Am I eligible? Available online at www.policecouldyou.co.uk/officers/eligible.html (accessed 10 March 2010).

Smith, R (2007) *Youth Justice Ideas, Policy, Practice*, 2nd edition. Cullompton: Willan.

Thomas, M (2008) Youth offending teams (YOTs), in Goldson, B (ed.) *Dictionary of Youth Justice*. Cullompton: Willan.

Walsh, C (2008) Curfew orders, in Goldson, B (ed.) *Dictionary of Youth Justice*, Cullompton: Willan.

Webster, C (2006) 'Race', youth crime and justice, in Goldson, B (ed.) *Youth Crime and Justice*. London: Sage.

FURTHER READING

Youth justice is an established part of the criminal justice system and the criminological literature, so there is no shortage of books and articles on the subject. Two comprehensive texts are Roger Smith's *Youth Justice Ideas, Policy, Practice* (2007) and John Muncie's *Youth and Crime* (2009), and both are highly recommended for those who wish to know more about the subject.

For those interested in restorative justice, both the above books contain sections on the subject, but the *Handbook on Restorative Justice* (ed. Johnstone, 2006), is recommended for those who wish to study it in greater depth.

USEFUL WEBSITES

www.direct.gov.uk/en/index.htm (Directgov, thewebsite of the UK government)

www.helptheaged.org.uk/en-gb/ (Help the Aged)

www.policecouldyou.co.uk/officers/eligible_details.html (Police: Could You?)

www.statewatch.org/asbo/ASBOwatch.htmlASBOwatch (ASBOwatch)

www.yjb.gov.uk/en-gb/yjb/Home.htm (Youth Justice Board)

3 Disability

By the end of this chapter you should be able to:

- outline the key national policy and legislation that relates to disability and is relevant to policing;
- describe at an introductory level some of the historical, criminological and sociological contexts relating to disability;
- reflect on the issues of dealing with disability in offenders, victims, witnesses and colleagues.

This chapter provides the following links to Skills for Justice, National Occupational Standards (NOS) for Policing and Law Enforcement 2008.

AB1   Communicate effectively with people.
BE2   Provide initial support to victims, survivors and witnesses and assess their need for further support.
CA1   Use law enforcement actions in a fair and justified way.
HB11   Promote equality of opportunity and diversity in your area of responsibility.

Introduction

Although people with disabilities have always been part of every human society, they have often been treated in an appallingly discriminatory and abusive way. It is only within the last two decades that there has been legislation to protect people with disabilities from discrimination, and policy recognition of the needs of this group by the police is even more recent. In this chapter, you will be introduced to the legislation on disability and will consider the distinctive nature of that legislation, which includes the concept of reasonable adjustment and allows discrimination in favour of people with disabilities. In the section on sociological and criminological theory you will consider the concept of social construction, which can be applied to all aspects of diversity but has particular relevance to disability. The discussion of police practice – past, present and future – will show the progression to a point where responding to disability hate crime is now a stated police priority. The chapter will also discuss mental health, dyslexia and learning difference, as well as the needs of police employees with disabilities.

Policy and legislation

It is perhaps surprising to note that, although legislation on racial equality and gender equality was introduced in the 1970s, it took until the mid-1990s before equality legislation related to disability was introduced. The primary legislation is the Disability Discrimination Act (DDA) 1995, which starts by defining disability. The Act describes a disabled person as someone having, or who has had in the past, a physical or mental impairment that has or had a substantial and long-term adverse effect on her or his ability to carry out normal day-to-day activities. The DDA 1995 provides protection for 'disabled persons' in recruitment, promotion, training, working conditions and dismissal.

Prior to the formation of the EHRC, the Disability Rights Commission (DRC) had a similar function to the Commission for Racial Equality (CRE) and Equal Opportunities Commission (EOC) for matters relevant to disability and had both an advisory and an enforcement role. In 2007 the DRC produced a draft Code of Practice for the DDA 1995 for employment and occupation. The new Code, like the previous ones, is not a legal document but could be used in evidence in legal proceedings. The Code clarified the new provisions, which significantly extend protection against disability discrimination to all workers (including paid and unpaid work placements) irrespective of the size of an organisation. The Code encompasses five main unlawful acts:

- to directly discriminate;

- to fail to undertake the duty to make a reasonable adjustment (direct discrimination) 'on the grounds of' disability;

- to carry out residual less favourable treatment 'for a disability-related reason';

- to carry out harassment;

- to carry out victimisation.

REFLECTIVE TASK

Reasonable adjustment

The law states that an employer has a duty to make reasonable adjustments to working conditions or to the physical working environment where that will overcome the practical effects of a disability. As Trevor Phillips notes (2008), the disability rights campaigners were among the first people in society to acknowledge that discrimination was not solely caused by individual bigots, but could be caused as much by a failure to act as by a specific action. The requirement on employers to make reasonable adjustment was a challenge to this.

For each of the examples below, would you consider the adjustment requested to be a reasonable one?

- *A suspect arrested on suspicion of burglary says that he will not consent to be interviewed unless his sister is present, as he is hearing impaired and he needs her to translate into sign language.*

- *A police officer with dyslexia asks to use voice-activated software to dictate reports, even though she is located in an open-plan office.*

- *A police officer with sleep apnoea makes a request to be excused from working night shifts as that aggravates the condition.*

- *A suspect in a serious violent offence has been remanded in custody. His mother is a wheelchair user and she presents to the local police station. As she is unable to travel to the prison, and access to the prison building itself is not easy, she requests that her son be brought to the local police station once a week so she could visit him there.*

The issue of risk assessments needs to be considered by reference to individual circumstances, without making stereotypical assumptions. A blanket approach would be viewed as directly discriminatory, unless it could be shown that no person with the disability in question could carry out the job concerned, even if reasonable adjustments were made. The Code makes reference to the 'Access to Work' scheme, which assists employers with funding for reasonable adjustments. It would be advisable to review disability awareness training to ensure a thorough understanding of legal obligations and the practice of reasonable adjustments. An audit of appraisal arrangements, any codes of conduct or policies relating to harassment and bullying, disciplinary/grievance procedures, and application of work–life balance policies may be required.

Larger employers, such as the police, need to consider whether there are any arrangements for consulting disabled employees over review of current policies and the impact of monitoring processes.

The Disability Discrimination Act 1995 (Amendment) Regulations 2003 came into force on 1 October 2004. Changes include amendments to definitions of discrimination and harassment. There is also a legal duty placed upon public sector bodies to actively promote disability equality.

The other significant point to note about the disability legislation is that it does not make it illegal to discriminate in favour of someone with a disability. It is therefore possible for employers to provide extra support for people with disabilities both at the recruitment stage and for current employees.

The Criminal Justice Act 2003 has now, in section 146, recognised the offence of disability hate crime, which is defined as a criminal offence motivated by hatred or prejudice towards a person due to their actual or perceived disability. It is a criminal offence when before, during or after a criminal offence a perpetrator demonstrates hatred towards a person due to their disability.

In 2007 the Home Office produced best practice guidance on *Disability in the Police Service*, which focuses particularly on the needs of employees and prospective employees with disabilities (Home Office, 2007).

Criminological and sociological perspectives

In other chapters we have started by outlining perspectives from criminological theory, but criminology has had little or nothing to say about most aspects of disability. However, disability has been considered by scholars in other social science disciplines and one theoretical framework that has particular insight into disability is that of 'social construction'. It can be a difficult theory to understand at first, but it is worth spending time on it as it provides insights into not just disability but all six strands of diversity.

The social construction of discrimination

As was discussed in the introduction, one of the perceived weaknesses of discussions framed in the language of diversity is that it can minimise the importance of power. It is argued by activists that it is not enough merely to acknowledge that there are many different groups in society; some of those groups are more powerful than others and this can lead to inequality and discrimination. An understanding of social construction, discourse and power is important to recognise the power relations within society. Clarke and Cochrane (1998) describe the process by which social problems are constructed as being concerned with 'the ways in which problems are identified, given meaning and acted upon'. In relation to the identification of social problems, they observe that these are considered to be 'social' in that they attract public attention, and are connected to concerns about wider issues such as justice and social order.

REFLECTIVE TASK

Giving meaning

Social construction can be a complicated concept, so perhaps these examples can help to explain it.

- *It used to be believed that certain jobs, such as that of a police officer, could only be done by men and not women. This was explained by reference to both physical and mental ability – that men were stronger and better at thinking quickly, so could fulfil the requirements of the job. Society and policing have changed, so we can now look back and see that these expectations were simply socially constructed – society had different expectations of men and women that were simply based on wrong assumptions having no basis in fact.*

- *It is often difficult for some people with physical disabilities to gain access to buildings. This is particularly the case in the criminal justice system where many buildings, such as courts, prisons and even some police stations, are quite old. Social construction is helpful in explaining this, as it demonstrates that the problem is not that a person is, say, a wheelchair user, but instead that the problem is that the designer of the building did not take into account that some people use wheelchairs.*

- *If a police officer was attempting to interview a witness to a crime who was hearing impaired and was unable to communicate, he or she might say, in frustration, that this was because the witness was deaf. An understanding of social construction would help the officer to explain that the interview was not possible because a sign language interpreter had not been made available.*

Try to come up with one further example to illustrate social construction. It is preferable, but not essential, that this example relates to disability and policing.

Discussing social problems is never straightforward, since all such debates are based on 'taken-for-granted' assumptions – what Clarke and Cochrane describe as 'what everybody knows' (1998, p10). This assumes the status of 'common sense' and relies on underlying theories and assumptions. Common sense has a powerful impact on discussions about social problems and Clarke and Cochrane (1998, p15) suggest that understanding 'common sense' is an essential feature of studying social problems. They identify three crucial aspects in this regard.

- Each bit of common sense involves a claim to be the truth – conflicting statements are not just different, they are contested in conflicts where each position seeks to be 'what everybody knows'.

- Common-sense views are connected to social and political action – for example, political parties often address 'common sense' in their efforts to persuade the public that their policies and answers are the right ones.

- These connections are important, since the dominance of some ideas over others (and the political articulation of some ideas) lead to and shape social action. That is, they have a direct consequence on the development of social policy through political initiatives.

Social construction therefore acts to produce and reproduce social order through the ways in which we identify, define and give meaning to social phenomena and enact our social constructions.

Common sense, 'everybody knows' and taken-for-granted assumptions

Read these statements.

- *A wheelchair user would not make an effective police constable.*

- *A member of the public who was visually impaired would not make a very good witness.*

- *An offender with a history of mental health problems is more likely to be dangerous than someone without that history.*

- *If someone with learning difficulties has been subject to verbal abuse for her whole life, insults will probably not affect her as she will be so used to them.*

All of these could be described as 'common sense'. Do you agree with each of these statements? Can you identify the assumptions behind them?

Hughes (1998) explores how social construction can apply to disability. He suggests that the medical model interprets disability in individual terms, and focuses on the impairment rather than the person. This invests power in the medical professions. However, the social model of disability challenges this by constructing disability as social oppression. Disability is constructed not in terms of a person's individual physical or mental impairments, but as a result of society being organised as if able-bodiedness is normal, resulting in structural difficulties for those with disabilities.

The criminal justice system

There are a number of different ways that disability discrimination can be evidenced in relation to the criminal justice system. These include:

- *failure to provide physical access to premises;*

- *failure to engage sign language interpreters;*

- *stereotyping of and prejudice against people with physical impairments, mental or learning difficulties.*

Can you think of any local examples that you have encountered?

Mental health

Although other aspects of disability have had little attention from criminology, there has been a long-standing interest in the link between offending and mental disorder. Although there are difficulties both in defining what is meant by mental disorder and in gathering statistics relating to the link between mental disorder and offending, it is clear that there is a higher incidence of mental disorder among offenders than there is among the rest of the population (Newburn, 2007; Canton, 2008). However, despite some media-generated fears that mental disorder is linked to violence, there is no evidence to suggest that mentally disordered offenders are any more violent than the rest of the offender population (Newburn, 2007).

Equally, another common mistake is to identify mental disorder in an offender and to then use it to explain all their offending, when in fact mentally disordered offenders offend for the same range of reasons as anyone else (Canton, 2008). The response to offending by people with mental disorders has been complicated, and sometimes confused, with the undesirable outcome of many people with mental disorders being detained in prison, due to the absence of any suitable alternatives (Newburn, 2007).

REFLECTIVE TASK

Mental health

If a police constable is called to an incident at a private home and is told that the alleged offender is a man with a mental disorder, how should the officer approach this incident? Should he or she prepare differently or behave differently than if there was no information about a mental disorder?

Historical and current police practice

It is only very recently that the police have given direct attention to the issue of disability, and in this section you will consider how aspects of health and disability have been considered by the police and the criminal justice system in general. Attention will be given to mental health, HIV/Aids and disability hate crime.

Disability hate crime

Disability hate crime has been considered as an issue somewhat belatedly, even though understanding of homophobic and racial hate crime has become well established (Roulstone et al., 2009). It is also considered in a different way – there has been no creation of a distinct offence of disability hate crime; under the Criminal Justice Act 2003 it is simply an aggravating factor in offences already available for prosecution. However, self-report studies, mainly carried out by campaigning agencies, have consistently found that bullying is prevalent towards people with disabilities, particularly learning disabilities, and that many have also been victims of vandalism, other property offences and assault.

There is some evidence that disability hate crime is increasing and that the groups most vulnerable to victimisation include those with mental health problems or learning difficulties (Chakraborti and Garland, 2009). Similarly to other forms of hate crime, the pattern of relatively low-level behaviour such as verbal abuse and harassment, which nevertheless has a serious cumulative impact, is also present in disability hate crime. This is particularly serious with regard to disability hate crime, as some victims may find such abuse particularly difficult to cope with.

The criminal justice system as a whole has been slow to respond to disability hate crime and even positive and constructive policies have sometimes foundered at an operational level. Reporting Centres were set up to combat the difficulties of police stations being hard to access, but these did not always remain operational and staff were sometimes inadequately trained (Roulstone et al., 2009). Those who did succeed in reporting the offences felt that they were not taken seriously. Courts have been reluctant to use the provisions under section 146 of the Criminal Justice Act, choosing instead to use their powers to sentence more severely for crimes committed against vulnerable groups. This has had the effect of reducing opportunities to publicise offences committed against people with disabilities (Chakraborti and Garland, 2009). The police have found it difficult to accept, first, that disabled people can be victims of hate crime and, second, that the offenders are often those who have responsibility for caring for the victims. This has led to a lack of confidence among the community of people with disabilities in the police's inclination and ability to investigate disability hate crime (Chakraborti and Garland, 2009).

PRACTICAL TASK

Disability hate crime

Two Leicestershire women, Fiona Pilkington and her 18-year-old daughter Francecca Hardwick, were found dead in their burnt-out car in October 2007. An inquest in 2009 found that Ms Pilkington had killed herself and her daughter. They had been subjected to a long history of regular and persistent abuse from local young people on account of Francecca's severe learning difficulties and her brother's severe dyslexia. The abuse included shouting obscenities, urinating in the garden and throwing stones and eggs at the windows.

The coroner at the inquest was very critical of the response of Leicestershire Constabulary. She questioned the assertion of the Assistant Chief Constable, who said that the police did not act as no prosecution could be brought as the incidents did not amount to crimes. The coroner suggested that, on the contrary, section 5 of the Public Order Act 1986 was one of seven or eight acts of Parliament that could have been used to bring a prosecution. At the time, Leicestershire Police did not recognise disability as a potential factor in hate crime, and also failed to link the individual incidents together.

In the next section we will consider how Leicestershire Constabulary has improved its practice since 2007.

HIV/Aids

Roulstone et al. (2009) identify the particular needs of people who are HIV positive. They do not fit neatly under the heading of disability, and are excluded from the statutory definition, but face prejudice and discrimination in all aspects of their lives. There is an association with homophobia, adding another dimension to this discrimination.

REFLECTIVE TASK

HIV/Aids in prison

One issue that is of particular relevance to offenders who are gay men is that of HIV/Aids in prison. In the UK, the main routes of transmission for the HI virus are through unprotected sex or needle exchange, so gay men and drug users are particularly vulnerable. (It is worth noting that this pattern is not repeated throughout the world; for example, in southern Africa, HIV is mainly transmitted via heterosexual relationships.) A Prison Reform Trust report in 2005 found that the HIV rate in prison was over 15 times that outside prison. However, prisons were providing sub-standard care. Over half of prisons did not have a sexual health policy. Prisoners did not have access to disinfectant, condoms, clean needles or information about health (Prison Reform Trust/National Aids Trust, 2005).

In 2006 responsibility for health in prison was transferred to the NHS. There is no research available on whether that has led to an improvement in the treatment of HIV-positive prisoners, but advice is available from the Citizen's Advice Bureau (CAB) (2009). It advises prisoners that there is no requirement that they undertake an HIV test on admission to prison, but they have the right to do so if they so choose. Condoms are available in prison, if the doctors think there is an infection risk, but there are no needle exchanges.

- *If a police officer arrested an offender who said that he or she was HIV positive, who should the police officer share that information with?*

- *If this offender expressed anxiety about going to prison and about possible bullying and access to medical treatment, how should the police officer advise the offender?*

Police staff and disability

The best practice guidelines for the police and disability are provided by the Home Office (2007) and deal with all aspects of employment, including recruitment, support of employees and promotion. The guidelines follow the principles of reasonable adjustment, and advise that these should be determined on an individual case-by-case basis. Police forces are advised to seek advice from specialists. Examples of what adjustments are considered reasonable are provided and include working hours, office conditions and workload demands. However, the recruitment policy acknowledges that the fitness requirements for police constables are non-negotiable as they are necessary for the safety of the public.

Best current police practice and plans for the future

Disability hate crime

Although the police have been criticised in the past for not taking disability hate crime seriously, or of developing specific policies to address it, the recognition of disability as one of the six strands of diversity has led to an increase in the attention given to the subject. Police forces have started by defining disability hate crime and the definition provided on the website of Leicestershire Constabulary is typical, and is also in line with the legislation. It defines disability hate crime as any incident that is perceived to be based upon prejudice towards or hatred of the victim because of their disability, or is so perceived by the victim or any other person (Leicestershire Constabulary, 2009).

The police, locally and nationally, have drawn in support from other bodies in responding to disability hate crime. Nationally, this includes the EHRC. Phillips (2008) identifies nine items relating to disability equality that the EHRC will focus on in the next few years. The second of these is disability hate crime. He, again, started from a position of referring to past police failings and identified two men, Brent Martin and Steven Hoskin, who were abused and then murdered due to their learning disabilities, and asserted that these cases should have been dealt with as disability hate crime.

One constabulary that has taken a local initiative is the Police Service of Northern Ireland, which joined with the Northern Ireland devolved government in commissioning a report on disability hate crime from the Institute for Conflict Research (ICR, 2009). It is suggested that the key findings from this research have relevance beyond Northern Ireland and they can be summarised as follows.

- People with disabilities reported a wide range of forms of hate crime that go well beyond what is reported to and recorded by the police. These instances include damage to property and both verbal and physical abuse.

- Although individuals were aware of the abuse that they face, they were much more likely to characterise it as bullying or harassment, rather than hate crime. Even people with disabilities themselves would often think of hate crime as something that happens to other groups. This was also true of many disability support organisations and even local police partnerships.

- There were many reasons given why disability hate crime is not always reported, but the most prominent of these is fear. The police have come up with creative ideas to increase the reporting rate, but these ideas need to address the fears of victims and witnesses.

- Disability hate crime rarely makes it through the judicial process, so the main criminal justice agency involved with it is the police. Greater awareness throughout the police, and better systems and processes, are required.

- The awareness of disability support agencies was low, and there was poor communication between them and criminal justice agencies.

- The awareness level from the general public of disability hate crime was low to non-existent. However, the police are currently undertaking an awareness campaign in schools.

The report also made some recommendations for improvement to police practice.

- The police should work with disability support organisations to set up protocols to allow disability hate crimes to be reported by third parties.

- The systems and processes of review and recording of disability hate crime should be reviewed against best practice standards.

- The police should ensure that Hate Incident Minority Liaison Officers (HIMLOs) are properly trained and aware of disability hate crime.

REFLECTIVE TASK

Disability hate crime policy

Leicestershire Constabulary did not have a disability hate crime policy in 2007, but now does have such a policy on its website (Leicestershire Constabulary, 2009). The policy encourages members of the public to contact the police immediately if they, or anyone they know, is being bullied as the result of a disability. The website provides advice on recording and reporting such incidents, and states that a Disability Hate Crime book is available.

- *Look again at the website of your own local police force. Does it have a policy on disability hate crime?*

- *If a member of the public was concerned about such a crime, could they easily find this information?*

Police staff and disability

The Home Office (2007) guidelines provide a list of reasons why police services should promote disability equality and these represent a strong rationale for compliance with the Disability Equality Duty.

- Disability equality makes business sense in recruitment, procurement and the provision of services.

- Disability equality helps the police to provide a better service to the public.

- Compliance with the Duty benefits all service users, not just those with disabilities.

- Police forces can make a real, positive change to the lives of those with disabilities, and this will increase the confidence that those people have in the work of the police.

- The police can provide better access to the public and, in turn, increase the public's involvement and participation.

- Compliance with the Duty brings advantages to the police in the recruitment and retention of staff; improvement in morale and staff management; potential to achieve a more representative workforce; and avoidance of claims of unlawful discrimination.

REFLECTIVE TASK

The Disability Equality Duty

- *The list of benefits above is a long one, but can you add anything to it? Can you think of any other reasons why police forces could or should promote disability equality?*

- *What is your own experience of how well the police have complied with the Disability Equality Duty?*

CHAPTER SUMMARY

In the same way as equality legislation relating to disability was introduced somewhat later than that relating to other aspects of diversity, the police have, perhaps, been slower to develop an approach to disability than they have to, say, race, religion or gender. However, as has been shown throughout this chapter, there are many aspects of disability that impact on police work, including mental health, HIV/Aids and, not least, the obligation to treat police staff with disabilities fairly and in line with the legislation. It is, however, the issue of disability hate crime that is likely to present the greatest and most high-profile challenge to policing in the next few years. Roulstone et al., writing early in 2009, say that:

> *A single event which captures the public imagination involving hatred of disabled people has not thankfully transpired, whilst the disabled peoples' movement has not to date cohered in a major way around hate crime and disability.*

(2009, p4)

But that may have changed since that article was written. It is likely that the attention given to the Fiona Pilkington case and the widespread anger and distress about what happened has led to the concept of disability hate crime entering the public consciousness. It is likely that, in the next few years, the police will be giving a lot of attention to the issue of disability hate crime.

Canton, R (2008) Working with mentally disordered offenders, in Green, S, Lancaster, E and Feasey, S (eds) *Addressing Offending Behaviour: Context, Practice and Values*. Cullompton: Willan.

Chakraborti, N and Garland, J (2009) *Hate Crime: Impact, Causes and Responses*. London: Sage.

Citizens Advice Bureau (CAB) *Health in Prison*. Available online at www.adviceguide.org.uk/p_health_in_prisons.pdf (accessed 15 August 2009).

Clarke, J and Cochrane, A (1998) The social construction of difference, in Saraga, E (ed.) *Embodying the Social: Constructions of Difference*. London: Routledge/Open University.

Home Office (2007) *Disability in the Police Service* guidance. Available online at http://police.homeoffice.gov.uk/publications/equality-diversity/disability-in-the-police-service/ (accessed 15 August 2009).

Hughes, G (1998) A suitable case for treatment? Constructions of disability, in Saraga, E (ed.) *Embodying the Social: Constructions of Difference*. London: Routledge/Open University.

Institute for Conflict Research (ICR) (2009) *Hate Crime against People with Disabilities*. Available online at www.conflictresearch.org.uk (accessed 15 August 2009).

Leicestershire Constabulary (2009) *Disability Hate Crime*. Available online at www.leics.police.uk/advice/5_support_for_victims/85_disability_hate_crime (accessed 10 March 2010).

Newburn, T (2007) *Criminology*. Cullompton: Willan.

Phillips, T (2008) Speech at the TUC Disability Conference. Available online at www.equalityhuman rights.com (accessed 15 August 2009).

Prison Reform Trust/National Aids Trust (2005) *HIV and Hepatitis in UK Prisons: Addressing Prisoners' Healthcare Needs*. Available online at www.prisonreformtrust.org.uk (accessed 15 August 2009).

Roulstone, A, Thomas, P, Balderston, S and Harris, J (2009) *Hate is a Strong Word: A Critical Policy Analysis of Disability Hate Crime in the British Criminal Justice System*. Edinburgh: Centre for Research on Families and Relationships.

FURTHER READING

There is much less written on policing and disability than on other aspects of diversity, but that is likely to change in the next few years, following the national attention given to the Pilkington case. For the moment, Roulstone et al.'s review, *Hate is a Strong Word* (2009), is a useful place to start reading about disability hate crime. The Home Office *Disability in the Police Service* guidance (2007) provides insight into the working environment for police officers with disabilities.

USEFUL WEBSITES

http://police.homeoffice.gov.uk/publications/equality-diversity/disability-in-the-police-service/ (Home Office's *Disability in the Police Service* guidance)

www.leics.police.uk/advice/5_support_for_victims/85_disability_hate_crime (Leicestershire Constabulary's *Disability Hate Crime*)

4 Gender

CHAPTER OBJECTIVES

By the end of this chapter you should be able to:

- outline the key national policy and legislation that relates to gender and is relevant to policing;
- describe at an introductory level some of the historical, criminological and sociological contexts relating to gender and policing;
- reflect on the issues of dealing with particular sorts of offending, such as sexual or domestic abuse.

LINKS TO STANDARDS

This chapter provides the following links to Skills for Justice, National Occupational Standards (NOS) for Policing and Law Enforcement 2008.

AB1 Communicate effectively with people.
BE2 Provide initial support to victims, survivors and witnesses and assess their need for further support.
CA1 Use law enforcement actions in a fair and justified way.
HB11 Promote equality of opportunity and diversity in your area of responsibility.

Introduction

The issue of gender is sometimes overlooked or minimised in discussions about diversity and equality. There is no doubt that great progress has been made in this area, both in policing and in wider society. Women are now employed in the police at all grades, up to Chief Constable, and undertake all policing tasks. Domestic abuse and sexual violence, which were once ignored or treated as simply private matters, are now central to the concerns of the police and other criminal justice agencies. However, it is still important to consider the issue of gender, as the police, and indeed most of the criminal justice system, with the exception of the Probation Service, remains extremely male dominated. It continues to be argued that male priorities dominate criminal justice policy and practice leading to, among other challenges, an unacceptably low conviction rate for some crimes against women. Some women police officers still report difficulties in integrating into the male-dominated police culture.

In this chapter the main policy and legislation relating to gender and policing will be briefly introduced. There is a general discussion on the insights that consideration of gender has brought to criminology and criminal justice, and how there have been changes in how women are viewed as offenders, victims and witnesses, as well as professionals and practitioners. The chapter then focuses on police practice, identifying challenges and criticisms, and on opportunities to replicate good practice.

Policy and legislation

Gender was one of the first strands of diversity to be dealt with in legislation. The Sex Discrimination Act (SDA) 1975 outlawed discrimination on the grounds of sex, while the SDA 1986 amended the SDA 1975 to ensure that discrimination related to retirement was covered by legislation.

The SDA 1975 cannot be looked at in isolation from other laws on equality. In particular, the Equal Pay Act (EPA) 1970 provides for equal pay for equal work for men and women. This is also affected by European law.

The position of transsexuals has been addressed by the Sex Discrimination (Gender Reassignment) Regulations 1999. The Regulations amend the SDA 1975 so as to provide that discrimination on the grounds of gender reassignment constitutes discrimination on the grounds of sex.

There is no one law against domestic abuse, but assault, criminal damage, harassment and attempted murder are all crimes. Likewise, sexual violence covers a wide range of activities, and rape and sexual assault are both criminal offences. The Domestic Violence, Crime and Victims Act 2004 has been enacted in stages since 2004 and provides added protection to victims. It extends the scope of the civil law to protect people in same-sex relationships and those who have never cohabited, and allows for a breach of a non-molestation order to be dealt with by arrest. An early evaluation of these provisions found inconsistencies and lack of clarity in the interpretation and operation of the legislation and recommended further police training (Ministry of Justice, 2008). This Act continues to have a staged rollout and, from 30 September 2009, the police have been given the powers to restrain offenders.

Criminological and sociological perspectives

Women as victims or offenders

The traditional role of women in the criminal justice system has been that of the victim, the witness and the family supporter. It is only comparatively recently that attention has been paid to women as offenders.

Early criminological theory was dominated by biological explanations of crime and women's offending was no different in being interpreted in that way. Women offenders were considered to be particularly primitive, cruel and evil. Although biological theories have long been discredited, such views of female offenders have been remarkably persistent. In addition, sociological explanations for offending tended to ignore the offending of women and girls, often assuming that all offenders were male. Later, criminologists became frustrated at the prejudices of the biologists and the ignorance of the sociologists and this led to the emergence of a feminist criminology (Newburn, 2007).

REFLECTIVE TASK

Feminism

This is the first time the word 'feminist' has been used in this book and it is a word that often has strong positive or negative associations for people:

> *More importantly, 'feminism' and 'feminists' have no place in the police organ-isation.*
>
> *(Silvestri, 2003, p10)*

What is your impression of the acceptance, or otherwise, of the term 'feminist' in the police?

Feminist criminologists (the most prominent writers are Carol Smart and Frances Heidensohn) sought to provide a more realistic assessment of female offending. Heidensohn (2007) argues that, towards the end of the twentieth century, one of the most significant developments in criminology was the realisation of the need to give attention to the relationship between gender and offending. She also argues that female offenders are:

- more likely to commit crimes motivated by economic rationality;
- less likely to reoffend or be violent;
- more likely to have their behaviour controlled by the criminal justice system;
- more likely to be stigmatised by the label of 'offender'.

A high-profile aspect of the consideration of women as offenders relates to women who kill their violent male partners. Campaigners have argued for some time that the definition of the legal defence of 'provocation' (which can reduce a murder charge to one of manslaughter and remove the requirement for a mandatory life sentence) favours men who are likely to act suddenly over women who might have been subjected to a lengthy period of cumulative provocation. Court of Appeal cases in the 1990s, including the well-known case of Sara Thornton, led to a reinterpretation of this law (Cavadino and Dignan, 2007).

Women also experience incarceration in a different way from men. Carlen and Worrall (2004) identify four themes that explain why women's prisons take the form that they do. The first theme of *prisonisation* explains how women take on the culture of the institution in which they are incarcerated. The second theme is in some tension with this, in that *resistance* explores how women resist the regime imposed. The third theme of *discrimination* shows that women are treated differently from men, but this often disadvantages them in that they are further from home and experience greater stigma. The fourth theme is known as *carceral clawback* and refers to ways in which security concerns can take precedence over attempts to make reforms to the prison regime.

The most comprehensive recent report on women and the criminal justice system is the Corston Report (Home Office, 2007). This report is mainly concerned with prisons and probation and its recommendations include the following.

- Every agency within the criminal justice system must prioritise gender equality.

- Small, locally based units should be introduced to replace existing women's prisons.

- There should be more strategic coordination of the pathways to resettlement.

- Custodial sentences for women should be restricted to serious and violent offenders, and this policy must be supported and explained by government.

The Corston Report focuses on prisons, but does have something to say about policing, particularly detention in police cells. The report recommends greater use of women's centres, better liaison between the police and the NHS regarding women in custody, and more timely psychiatric assessment.

Feminist criminologists have also sought to highlight the experience of women as victims and witnesses. One common theme throughout the criminal justice system is how women are affected by traditional stereotypical ideas about gender. A prominent example of this, described by leading barrister Helena Kennedy (1993), is the Jeffrey Archer libel trial (see the Reflective task below). Kennedy's point is that the credibility of women's testimony in court is often judged not on the basis of the information provided, but on whether they are perceived to be 'good' or 'bad' women. In addition, the 'good wife', with her children, is often a hidden victim of the criminal justice system, for whom a spouse's term of imprisonment means: 'the loneliness of separation, bringing up a family without support, suffering financial hardship and the misery of long journeys and unfulfilling visits to remote prisons' (Kennedy, 1993, p65).

REFLECTIVE TASK

Jeffrey Archer, Mary Archer and Monica Coghlan

Jeffrey Archer, the millionaire author and former chairman of the Conservative Party, won a case for libel after the judge in the case contrasted his 'fragrant' wife Mary with the prosecution witness, prostitute Monica Coghlan. It was subsequently established that Archer had lied during the trial and he served a prison sentence for perjury.

- *Use Kennedy (1993) or other sources to find out more about this case. Do you think that gender assumptions led to the wrong verdict being returned?*

Kennedy's (1993) view is that criminal justice professionals (including judges, lawyers and police officers) are often less concerned with the facts of the crime than assessing the character of the woman before them.

Crimes in which women have been victims, such as rape, sexual assault and violence, have historically received little attention from the criminal justice system. Feminist criminology has contributed significantly to the increasing visibility of these sorts of offences, as well as the realisation that power is an important component in interpreting this offending, and that women can be at greater risk in the home than outside it. Feminist criminologists have also challenged the criminal justice system to take these sorts of offences seriously, and to appreciate that failing to support victims and/or prosecute offenders can be experienced by female victims as if a further offence has been committed against them – a process known as 'secondary victimisation'. The steps taken to address this are discussed in the next section, along with other factors in the development of police practice in relation to gender.

Women in the workplace

We will go on to consider the experiences that women have had as employees of police organisations, but it is important to consider this in the wider context of women's experience of employment in general. At the time of writing the EHRC is carrying out a consultation into the role of women in the workplace and the gender pay gap. The Commission states that this consultation is needed as, even 40 years after the Equal Pay Act, the gender pay gap is 22.6 per cent (EHRC, 2009). It is their view that greater transparency about pay, particularly in the private sector, will help to address this. Earlier research by the Commission (EHRC, 2009) found that the main factors that led to this pay gap were as follows.

- *Household division of labour*. Women tend to take on a greater burden of domestic duties than men, particularly those related to the care of young children, and this can have a detrimental effect on their career development.

- *Occupational concentration.* There are still many professions, or roles within professions, that are dominated by one gender or another. Professions dominated by men (for example, the fire or prison services) tend to be better paid than similar professions dominated by women (such as probation or social work).

- *The impact of motherhood.* Motherhood affects whether women work at all, what hours they work and the pattern of their work.

- *The low pay of part-time work.* It is still the case that part-time work is lower paid than full-time work, and there has been little change in this over the past 30 years.

- *The undervaluing of work traditionally performed by women.* Some of the lowest paid work in the country, such as cleaning, is mainly carried out by women.

- *Pay discrimination*. There are still some aspects of the pay gap that simply cannot be explained by the factors above. It is possible that there is still direct discrimination from some employers, who will pay men more than women, simply because of their gender.

Although there are some specific factors relating to police culture that explain the difference in pay and prospects between women and men in the police, it is important to note that the police are not unusual in this respect; the gender pay gap is a fact throughout society.

Media representations

As with some other aspects of diversity (particularly sexual orientation), the significant advances in society over a short period of time can serve to mask how much has changed, or how different life was just a few years ago. Media representations can illuminate life in society only a few years ago, and can show social change in a clear and engaging way. Watching television programmes from a particular era will illustrate the norms of that society.

The American programme Bewitched *clearly shows life in 1950s' USA, where women stayed at home and men went to work. Another American programme,* Cagney and Lacey, *and the British programme,* Juliet Bravo, *portrayed the lives of women police officers at a time when it was still generally considered to be a 'man's job'.*

Although these programmes are not shown much nowadays, there is a trend for modern programmes to be set in the past. Mad Men *portrays the challenges facing women in 1960s' America as they start to move out of the home and out of stereotypical female jobs (receptionists, secretaries, telephone operators) into more significant jobs.* Life on Mars *and* Ashes to Ashes *portray policing in the 1970s and 1980s, with some dramatic licence along the way, but do demonstrate an illuminating contrast with the modern police workplace.*

Track down and watch an episode of Ashes to Ashes.

- *What would be the advantages and disadvantages, for both women and men, of working in an environment such as that portrayed in* Ashes to Ashes, *as compared to the modern police workplace?*

Historical and current police practice

For most of the nineteenth century all police recruits were required to be male. The First World War provided an impetus for the recruitment of women into the police force and the first policewoman in the UK was appointed early in the twentieth century. Early police women tended to be middle-class volunteers who carried out quite specialist roles within the force, including monitoring the moral behaviour of other women, air-raid duty and controlling drug-trafficking to soldiers. Following the end of the war most police forces in England and Wales employed very few, if any, women, and restricted them to quite narrow duties.

The Second World War meant that most forces had to recruit women again and it was at that point that the long, slow process of giving female officers similar duties to male officers began (Rawlings, 2002). A main driver in the acceleration of female recruitment into the police was the sex discrimination legislation of the 1970s, outlined in the first section of this chapter. The introduction of this legislation reflected the changes in British society at that time, with a growing expectation that all aspects of employment should be open to both men and women.

Throughout the twentieth century there was an increasing number of women appointed at all grades in the police, culminating in the appointment of the first female Chief Constable, Pauline Clare, in 1995. Women currently make up approximately one-fifth of the ranks of all police officers and have a higher representation in other grades, such as PCSOs, special constables and civilian support staff. In both the UK and the USA the movement to increase the employment of women in the police was connected to campaigns to increase female representation in other criminal justice institutions, such as prisons, and to improve the treatment of women by the criminal justice system (Heidensohn, 2007).

The police responded to the changes in society and the changes in legislation, rather than leading the change, and Heidensohn (2007) has identified the following four themes emerging from the integration of women into the police since the 1970s.

Models of equality

Particularly in the early stages of integration, women were judged on whether they could undertake police tasks as well as men. Female officers often found that they needed to prove their ability by successfully undertaking a traditional police task, such as making an arrest. In more recent years police tasks are starting to be conceptualised in a more gender-neutral way. Women are outperforming men in some ways, for example female applicants consistently do better in assessment centres for sergeants and inspectors.

Coming to terms with police culture

Some of the good practice in the integration of women police officers into the police is described below in the section on best current practice. However, Heidensohn (2007) also identifies some difficulties, such as the case of Alison Halford, and her own research found that women often fell back on professionalism and a sense of mission to cope with an often hostile culture.

CASE STUDY

In the early 1990s Alison Halford, an Assistant Chief Constable in Merseyside Police, claimed that she had been passed over for further promotion because she was a woman. She won the case, proving sexual discrimination against the police. In addition, Halford won a case in the European Court of Human Rights, which found that her privacy had been breached, in violation of article 8 of the European Convention, when her phone calls were intercepted by senior officers. This case has been described as having huge

CASE STUDY continued

significance for the police, revealing not just the prevailing police culture, but also the discomfort felt by some people when faced with a woman in a position of power (Walklate, 2004).

Notwithstanding the increase in numbers of women police officers, the police remains a male-dominated institution, in number and, more arguably, in ethos. Heidensohn (2007) argues that, in contrast to other parts of the criminal justice system, and other criminological discourses, the police have always been conscious of gender, albeit in a very explicit male way. She describes such aspects of police practice as the use of violence and aggression to exert authority and the emphasis on unquestioned loyalty as explicitly masculine. Heidensohn is one of a number of writers who characterise the institution of the police as a 'world of old-fashioned machismo'. Silvestri (2003) uses Charles Handy's model of the four Greek gods of management to characterise police culture as a bureaucratic, hierarchical, 'Apollo' role culture, where authority is associated with an individual's position in the hierarchy. Other writers have cited this macho culture as being responsible for some of the difficulties and challenges faced by the police in recent years and decades. Smith and Gray (1985) describe the culture as being similar to that of a rugby club or boys' school, leading to an acceptance and even glamorisation of violence. Skolnick and Fyfe (1993) identified the macho culture of the Los Angeles Police Department (LAPD) as a factor leading to the assault on Rodney King, a black man arrested after a car chase.

Heidensohn (2007) reflects that, although most practitioners and academics who have studied police culture have noted the 'macho' element of the organisation, they have not always considered it to be a problem. Waddington (1999), for example, says that the main complaint that women police officers have is that they are sometimes not permitted to carry out 'real police work'. He argues that police subculture should be understood as functional and defensive, and necessary for a group of professionals carrying out a difficult and dangerous job on the margins of society. However, whether commentators approve or disapprove of this 'macho' culture, it is significant that they do have to engage with the issue of gender.

REFLECTIVE TASK

Old-fashioned machismo

- *What do you understand by the phrase 'a world of old-fashioned machismo'?*

- *Can you think of any environment that you have encountered that could be described in that way? It does not have to be a workplace; it could be a sports team, a social venue or even a small group of friends or relations.*

REFLECTIVE TASK *continued*

- *As a student of policing, is it your impression that your local police occupy a 'world of old-fashioned machismo'?*

- *Think of your favourite police television show: is the police environment portrayed in this way there? What effect might this have on police recruitment?*

Banks (2004) also discusses police culture and gender in her discussion of the 'ethics of care'. Banks proposes the ethics of care as a way of helping professionals resolve practical ethical dilemmas, rather than becoming stuck in a prolonged consideration of whether to take a deontological or consequentialist approach to ethical dilemmas, as discussed in Chapter 1. Her characterisation of the ethics of care is that decisions should be made on the basis of caring for others. In society, caring roles have traditionally been carried out by women, so, as an organisation such as the police employs more women, it is likely to take a more caring approach. Women are more inclined to make decisions based on relationships, rather than rules and principles, and this will have an impact on the organisation.

REFLECTIVE TASK

Caring women

- *It is asserted above that women are more inclined than men to be caring and to prioritise relationships. Do you agree with this?*

- *It has been suggested by some that this might be as a result of biological differences, while others believe that the more caring approach taken by women is socially constructed. Do you have a view on this? What is your view and why?*

Careers

Women are now much more likely to consider the police as a career, and their promotion prospects are as good as, or even better than, men. Women are more likely to choose roles that bring them into contact with child victims, while men are more drawn to roles associated with cars and guns. Although in the past the tendency to place women in specialist child protection or domestic abuse units might have been detrimental to their careers, Heidensohn and Gelsthorpe (2007) have suggested that the increasing prominence given to these specialisms may now actually put some women officers in an advantageous position. Women are now being promoted to the very highest ranks of the police, but women in very senior positions are still in a small minority and can find themselves isolated.

PRACTICAL TASK

Senior women officers

- *Find out who are the most senior women police officers in England and Wales.*

- *Find out who are the most senior officers in the area where you work or study.*

- *What is the ratio of women to men in senior positions, both locally and nationally?*

As discussed above, it is still the case throughout society that women earn less than men and are under-represented in the best-paid and most influential posts. Marisa Silvestri investigated why that was specifically the case in the police. She identified that there were particular characteristics about police culture, and particularly expectations related to promotion, that made it much harder for women than men to achieve promotion.

- *Time*. Silvestri (2003) estimates that the average police career lasts about 30 years, which appears to provide ample time for promotion to high rank. However, it is more revealing to think of aspiring Chief Constables who are promoted to Sergeant in their late twenties as having 20 years to achieve seven further promotions. This usually requires a few quick promotions at an early stage, and this can count against women who take time out for maternity and childcare reasons. Many women identify the need to balance the competing demands of work and family as the key factor in determining a decision not to apply for promotion. Women who are keen to pursue career aspirations find themselves opting to return to work after maternity leave sooner than they would otherwise choose and women who decide to work part-time find that more senior positions in the organisation are very rarely open to part-time or job-share options. In addition, women are less inclined than men to think about their future career in a planned and strategic way, so may miss out on opportunities for promotion in the early part of their careers.

- *Place*. Although many of the factors that lead to an under-representation of women in senior positions are common to many organisations, there are some that are distinct to the police. One of these is the expectation that senior officers will have worked in a variety of roles and in more than one constabulary. Women are disproportionately allocated to work with women and children, and this is often seen as being of low status. Women with children may find it hard to accommodate the demands of some high-status work, such as intelligence gathering, as its demands do not fit in well with part-time working. In addition, the expectation that officers intending to apply for senior posts will work in more than one constabulary will cause difficulties for women with children due to the detrimental impact this can have on family life.

Employment prospects

Suhama is a police constable in her early twenties. For as long as she can remember she has always wanted to be a police officer, and is now delighted to be fully qualified and on operational duties. She holds a Foundation Degree in Police Studies and the tutors and trainers on that course identified her as an exceptional student with great potential. When asked about her future career plans, Suhama says that she has not really thought too far ahead, but she cannot imagine working anywhere else than the police and hopes to spend many years in the organisation. Suhama has recently married and intends to start a family as soon as possible.

William is also a police constable in his early twenties, and a colleague of Suhama. He completed the same FD as Suhama and, by his own admission, cruised through the course at about 60 per cent of maximum possible effort, never achieving high marks but never in danger of failing either. He is, however, ambitious to do well in his career and aims to achieve a high rank. William realises that qualified and experienced police officers can have many opportunities open to them, and accepts that he may have to leave the police at some stage to maximise his earning potential. When asked about his plans for a family, William says that he is far too young to think about such matters.

- *What do you think is likely to happen to Suhama and William in their careers?*

- *In ten years' time, who is likely to be earning more?*

- *Should the police be making particular efforts to support either, both or neither of these officers?*

- *If Suhama and William came to you for careers advice, how might you advise them?*

New agendas

As society's priorities have changed over the last few decades, this has also been the case for the police, and some of these changes have a direct link to gender issues. The main instances of these changes relate to violence against women and children, in sexual abuse, sexual violence and domestic abuse. Until the 1970s the police were very reluctant to get involved in matters of domestic or sexual violence, characterising them as domestic matters, and not appropriate to be dealt with under criminal law. Women were not treated sympathetically and were either blamed, explicitly or implicitly, for what had happened, or were advised to change their behaviour to avoid a repeat. Rape victims were unwilling to go to the police because of fear that they would be disbelieved or even bullied.

The police have increasingly improved their practice of treating victims sympathetically (although see the Case study below for an outline of the criticisms in the Victoria Climbié case) and are now tending to take an inter-agency approach. Women tend to gravitate towards posts in these teams, and the increasing emphasis on community work in policing can also be connected to the increase in the number of women police officers employed, and their increasing influence on the priorities of the force.

CASE STUDY

Victoria Climbié died in 2000, in Haringey, following horrific abuse and neglect by her family, who should have been caring for her. Lord Laming led the inquiry into her death and criticised all the agencies involved. With regard to the police, he found that child protection teams were treated as 'Cinderella services', with insufficient attention or resources. He found deficiencies in staff training, staff levels, accommodation and equipment. He recommended that the Home Office and the police give much greater priority to child protection (Laming, 2003).

In 2009, following the preventable death of another child in Haringey, Peter Connelly (initially known as 'Baby P'), Lord Laming repeated his recommendations for improvement in the resourcing of child protection and the training of police child protection teams (Laming, 2009).

Date rape

Another aspect of police practice that received a lot of criticism in the past was their response to so-called 'date rape'. Walklate (2004) has listed some of the assumptions that have prevailed in society about rape and that have influenced the response of the criminal justice system.

- 'A woman runs faster with her knickers up than a man with his trousers down.'
- Stranger rape is 'real' rape.
- Women frequently make up allegations of rape.
- Rape only occurs out of doors.
- A prostitute cannot be raped.
- When a woman says 'no' she really means 'yes'.

The prevalence of these myths has affected the willingness of women to report date rape, the willingness of the police and Crown Prosecution Service (CPS) to prosecute, and the decisions of juries. This becomes a vicious cycle: if juries will not convict, the CPS becomes even less likely to prosecute and women become even less likely to report offences, resulting in the incredibly low conviction rate for offences of rape. Around 6.5 per cent of rape offences result in a conviction, compared to 34 per cent of criminal cases in general.

Feminist campaigners have had some success both in challenging the assumptions and in changing the law. Kennedy (1993) and others have successfully challenged the view that women who consent to a dinner or a cup of coffee have also consented to sex, but in individual court cases these sorts of interpretation can easily be drawn. From a legal point of view, the Criminal Justice and Public Order Act 1994 and the Sexual Offences Act 2003 both widened the definition of rape, thus providing greater protection to victims.

Best current practice and plans for the future

The Gender Agenda

In the UK the best practice on gender and policing is led by the British Association of Women Police and their Gender Agenda. The Agenda started in 2000 and 2001 as women police officers sought to highlight the working environment as they experienced it, and to promote and publicise best practice. The original Gender Agenda set out five long-term aims.

1. For the service to demonstrate consistently that it values women officers.

2. To achieve a consistent and proportionate gender, ethnic and sexual orientation balance across all ranks and specialisms.

3. To have a woman's voice on all influential policy forums.

4. To develop an understanding of the competing demands of having a good work–life balance and a successful career in the police.

5. To achieve a working environment that allows women to do their job professionally and consistently.

This document has been updated and reviewed since 2000, most notably in 2006, but the long-term aims have remained consistent. The Gender Agenda has produced literature, training material and events, and continues to play an important role in promoting the interests of women in the police. Importantly, in 2006 the scope of the Agenda, relaunched as Gender Agenda 2, was expanded to include all staff employed by the police. At that time progress against the five long-term aims was measured and, although a lot had been achieved, the organisation had not yet fully achieved equality of opportunity. The British Association for Women in Policing (BAWP) suggested that there were four main reasons for this.

- There was continuing perpetuation of myths and stereotypes about women.

- Flexible working opportunities were not being offered routinely.

- The female perspective was not being taken into account in policy development.

- The impact of the majority group culture on minority groups was not properly appreciated.

The organisation also identified and publicised positive initiatives at that time, with a view to encouraging their replication. These examples included good practice in promoting other aspects of diversity, such as the employment policies of the Police Service of Northern Ireland, which could be adapted to promote gender equality as well. Promoting and publicising good practice has been an enduring characteristic of the BAWP (see the

Practical task below). Throughout this book it has been consistently stated that good diversity practice does not simply support the particular group being discussed at that time, but brings benefit to the whole organisation. Gender Agenda 2 embraces that principle and explicitly states the benefits that gender equality will have for the entire police service.

- Women currently make up only 22 per cent of the police force, despite constituting 50 per cent of the population. A balanced workforce is the best way to support and police the community.

- Police policies must be gender-proofed, to provide police services to both women and men and to attract both men and women to consider the police as a potential employer.

- It is crucial that the police must stop wasting potential and failing to use available expertise.

- Taking proactive action with regard to gender equality will prevent the need for employment tribunals.

- Flexible approaches to working practices and work–life balance brings benefits to individuals and to the organisation as a whole.

Currently, the BAWP is using training courses and drama initiatives to promote its aims and, through its website, encourages and supports women of all grades in the police. It produces regular newsletters and, in 2009, was continuing to campaign for appropriate uniforms and to highlight successes such as increases in flexible working and the achievements of individual female officers.

PRACTICAL TASK

Good practice

One of the documents produced through Gender Agenda 2 is a collation of good practice from police forces throughout the UK (BAWP, 2007). This document can be found at www.bawp.org/assets/file/GA2%20GP%20document%20current.pdf.

- *For each of the five long-term aims identified at the beginning of this section, try to identify one example of good practice that you find particularly striking, and would like to see replicated more widely.*

- *What steps could you, as an individual, or with a group of colleagues, take to ensure that best practice is replicated in your local constabulary?*

Although the BAWP takes a collaborative and inclusive approach, others have been more forthright in arguing that there are some aspects of policing that are carried out better by women than by men. Heidensohn argues that the traditional macho police culture is no longer fit for purpose in the twenty-first century:

> *The protective agenda has not disappeared and indeed has gained new importance in the twenty-first century with concerns about domestic violence, child abuse and sexual assaults. How these matters should be policed, who should do it, how offenders are dealt with, are high profile topics for all law enforcement agencies.*

> (2007, p575)

The American equivalent of the BAWP, the National Center for Women and Policing (NCWP), has produced research (NCWP, 2002) that suggests that female officers are much less likely to use excessive force than male officers. Male officers are more likely to have allegations of excessive force made against them, more likely to have these allegations upheld, and more likely to have liability lawsuits paid out against them. As the report points out, use of excessive force by the police does not just cost the force money, it undermines trust between the police and the community. The report suggests that an explanation for this difference could be the inclination of female officers to attempt to resolve situations by communication and conciliation, and being slower than their male colleagues to resort to the use of force.

Domestic abuse and sexual violence

There is a clear relationship between the recruitment and retention of female officers and the way that the police have responded to domestic abuse and sexual violence. This relationship is not straightforward; it is not the case that simply recruiting more women automatically leads to better treatment for victims. However, the trends in society that have led to an increasing acceptance of women in the police have also led to increasing attention being given to how these types of offences are dealt with.

Throughout the 1980s and 1990s police circulars were issued, to Chief Constables and then to forces, moving domestic abuse to a more central position in police priorities. Police forces were required to have policies on domestic abuse and these policies were required to include the following.

- The overriding duty to protect the women and children involved from further abuse.

- The need to treat domestic abuse just as seriously as other violence is treated.

- The use of the power to arrest.

- The danger of promoting reconciliation between the perpetrator and the victim.

- The need to have adequate and effective recording and monitoring systems.

Many forces employed specialist officers in Family Protection Units and Domestic Violence Units, although some of these units were subsequently disbanded. It is increasingly the practice in both the USA and the UK to deal with domestic abuse by arrest, which has an obvious effect on police practice, but the evidence is inconclusive on whether this is effective, or is what victims want. However, the impact of the legal changes, combined with the high-profile change in police practice, has been that a clear message has been sent that the police now treat domestic abuse incidents very seriously.

Women's Aid contrast the current police response to domestic abuse to that before the 1980s, praising the more serious approach taken to these offences and the improved communication between the police and other agencies. Walklate (2004) identifies two themes in the recent police response to domestic abuse: a tendency to use female officers and the focus on supporting the women and children. This has had a generally positive effect on police practice in this area, although there is a long way to go before it can be definitively stated that women have been empowered. However, this work is still not seen as high status within police organisations, and the allocation of women officers to these units can be a factor in limiting the careers of these officers (Westmarland, 2002).

REFLECTIVE TASK

'Not real police work'

In discussions on domestic abuse and policing it is regularly asserted that domestic abuse cases have a low status in the police and that officers are reluctant to engage in this work. For example, Walklate (2004) relates interviews with officers, both male and female, who consider work with women victims, carried out by women officers, to be 'not real police work'.

- *Why are these attitudes and beliefs likely to be held and what could be done to change this?*

Brown and Heidensohn (2000) found in their international research that the improvement in attitudes about rape was greater than that relating to domestic abuse, and found a connection between how progressive a force was in employing women and how well it dealt with victims of sexual assault. The policing of sexual assault encounters the same tension as that discussed in relation to domestic abuse: the use of female officers has improved the service given to women and children as victims, and has increased the profile of this work, but has led to it being seen as 'women's work' and 'not real police work', and has thus limited the careers of those who work in the specialist units. It seems to be accepted that women are the appropriate officers to deal with victims who are women and children but, as Westmarland states, 'To what extent this is led by preferences of victims, public demand, or a traditional belief in the "natural" caring abilities of female officers, is difficult to quantify' (2002, p57).

As Goldstein (2005) points out, however, responding appropriately to rape and sexual violence involves more than simply responding to complaints. It also includes crime prevention initiatives, such as providing education, transport, safe lighting and support services.

Police attitudes to victims of sexual violence have improved markedly in the UK, although there remain troubling questions to be answered about some cases (see the Case study below). The increasing representation of women at all grades of the police will not in itself be sufficient to ensure that domestic and sexual violence offences are properly dealt with, but it is an important factor in ensuring that it remains an important policing priority.

Rape

The Inspectorates of the Constabulary and the CPS (HMIC and HMCPSI) published a joint thematic report on the investigation and prosecution of rape cases in 2002. This report made recommendations and suggestions to improve the treatment of rape victims by the police and to improve the records of both the police and the CPS in successfully prosecuting rape cases. This led to the government's publication of a Rape Action Plan. However, despite these measures and the changes in legislation, the attrition rate for rape cases remained high, and a follow-up report was produced in 2007. This report estimated that between 75 and 95 per cent of rape cases were not reported to the police. This report made 12 recommendations, of which six related to police practice.

- Police forces specifically include the auditing of rape 'no crimes' within their auditing processes.

- Police forces review the use of Specially Trained Officers (STOs) to ensure that they are properly trained and supervised, with manageable workloads.

- Police forces issue guidance to first response officers on action to be taken in responding to a rape, including taking an initial victim's account.

- The Association of Chief Police Officers (ACPO), along with the CPS, should revisit the processes for taking victims' statements in rape cases, taking into account the evaluation of pilot schemes.

- Police forces should review rape investigations and monitor the quality of those reviews.

- When expert advice is sought from a forensic psychologist, all information should be sent to that expert as soon as possible.

CASE STUDY

A recent example highlighting the challenges of investigating rape allegations is that of John Worboys. He was a London taxi driver who, in 2009, was convicted of 19 charges, including some of rape and sexual assault. At the time of writing, the police handling of this case is being investigated by the Independent Police Complaints Commission (IPCC) at the request of the Metropolitan Police Service (MPS). Worboys was arrested following a complaint in 2007, but was released following interview. He went on to commit further offences. The police have faced considerable criticism from the media for their failure to arrest and charge Worboys sooner, despite receiving complaints as early as 2002. Guardian journalist Joan Smith's (2009) statement is representative of some of the coverage:

> *other men will go on attacking women until the criminal justice system and the popular press stop accepting offenders' excuses and start believing their victims.*

REFLECTIVE TASK

Rape conviction rates

- Do you think that the six recommendations outlined in this section will improve the conviction rate for rape?

- Can you think of any further steps that could be taken?

C H A P T E R   S U M M A R Y

In this chapter the history of women in the criminal justice system has been considered, with particular reference to the employment of women in the police and the response of the police to offences of particular concern to women, such as domestic and sexual violence. It is clear that much has been achieved, with women now employed at every grade of the police force, and domestic and sexual violence now dealt with as serious criminal offences. The objectives set as part of the Gender Agenda (see pages 70–2) are a reminder that much is still to be achieved, but the campaigning efforts of the BAWP, and others, will ensure that the importance of these objectives will be acknowledged throughout the police.

REFERENCES

Banks, C (2004) *Criminal Justice Ethics*. Thousand Oaks, CA: Sage.

British Association for Women in Policing (BAWP) (2007*) Gender Agenda 2: Good Practice*. Available online at www.bawp.org/assets/file/GA2%20GP%20document%20current.pdf (accessed 15 August 2009).·

Brown, J and Heidensohn, F (2000) *Gender and Policing*. Basingstoke: Macmillan.

Carlen, P and Worrall, A (2004) *Analysing Women's Imprisonment*. Cullompton: Willan.

Cavadino, M and Dignan, J (2007) *The Penal System: An Introduction*, 4th edition. London: Sage.

Equality and Human Rights Commission (EHRC) (2009) *Pay Gaps across the Equality Strands: A Review*. Available online at www.equalityhumanrights.com/fairer-britain/gender-pay-reporting/ (accessed 15 August 2009).

Goldstein, H (2005) Improving policing: a problem-oriented approach, in Newburn, T (ed.) *Policing: Key Readings*. Cullompton: Willan.

Heidensohn, F (2007) Gender and policing, in Newburn, T (ed.) *Handbook of Policing*. Cullompton: Willan.

Heidensohn, F and Gelsthorpe, L (2007) Gender and crime, in Maguire, M, Morgan, R and Reiner, R (eds) *The Oxford Handbook of Criminology*. Oxford: Oxford University Press.

Her Majesty's Inspectorate of Constabulary/Her Majesty's Crown Prosecution Service Inspectorate (HMIC/HMCPSI) (2002) *Allegations of Rape: Thematic Report*. Available online at http://inspectorates. homeoffice.gov.uk/hmic/inspections/thematic/aor/ (accessed 15 August 2009).

Her Majesty's Inspectorate of Constabulary/Her Majesty's Crown Prosecution Service Inspectorate (HMIC/HMCPSI) (2007) *Without Consent*. Available online at http://inspectorates.homeoffice.gov.uk/hmic/inspections/thematic/wc-thematic/them07-wc.pdf?view=Binary (accessed 15 August 2009).

Home Office (2007) *The Corston Report: A Review of Women with Particular Vulnerabilities in the Criminal Justice System*. London: Home Office. Available online at www.homeoffice.gov.uk/documents/corston-report/ (accessed 15 August 2009).

Kennedy, H (1993) *Eve Was Framed*. London: Chatto & Windus.

Laming, Lord H (2003) *The Victoria Climbié Inquiry Report*. London: HMSO. Available online at www.victoria-climbie-inquiry.org.uk/finreport/report.pdf (accessed 15 August 2009).

Laming, Lord H (2009) *The Protection of Children in England: A Progress Report*. London: HMSO. Available online at http://news.bbc.co.uk/1/shared/bsp/hi/pdfs/12_03_09_children.pdf (accessed 15 August 2009).

Ministry of Justice (2008) *Early Evaluation of the Domestic Violence, Crime and Victims Act 2004*. London: Ministry of Justice. Available online at www.justice.gov.uk/publications/docs/domestic-violence-report-2004.pdf (accessed 15 March 2010).

National Center for Women and Policing (NCWP) (2002) *Men, Women and Police Excessive Force*. Available online at www.womenandpolicing.org/PDF/2002_Excessive_Force.pdf (accessed 15 August 2009).

Newburn, T (2007) *Criminology*. Cullompton: Willan.

Rawlings, P (2002) *Policing: A Short History*. Cullompton: Willan.

Silvestri, M (2003) *Women in Charge: Policing, Gender and Leadership*. Cullompton: Willan.

Skolnick, J and Fyfe, J (1993) *Above the Law*. New York: Wiley.

Smith, D and Gray, J (1985) *Police and People in London* (The PSI Report). Aldershot: Gower.

Smith, J (2009) Soft on rape, soft on the causes of rape. *The Guardian*, 15 March. Available online at www.guardian.co.uk/commentisfree/2009/mar/15/ukcrime-justice (accessed 15 August 2009).

Waddington, P A J (1999) Police (canteen) sub-culture: an appreciation. *British Journal of Criminology*, 39(2): 286–309.

Walklate, S (2004) *Gender, Crime and Criminal Justice*. Cullompton: Willan.

Westmarland, L (2002) *Gender and Policing*. Cullompton: Willan.

FURTHER READING

The most prominent writer on gender and policing is Frances Heidensohn and her chapter in the *Handbook of Policing* (ed. Newburn, 2007) should be a starting point for anyone who wishes to study this subject further. The BAWP website (see below) contains a wealth of information, including a reference library, and the Women's Aid website contains extensive information about domestic abuse of use both to professionals and the wider community.

If you would like to read about gender and police careers in more depth, Marisa Silvestri's book, *Women in Charge* (2003), contains interesting interviews and excellent analysis.

www.bawp.org/index.php (British Association for Women in Policing)

www.equalityhumanrights.com/ (Equality and Human Rights Commission)

www.womenandpolicing.org/ (National Center for Women and Policing)

www.womensaid.org.uk/default.asp (Women's Aid)

5 Race

Introduction

Although all strands of diversity are important and relevant to policing, it is the issue of race and racism that has received the most attention and has, arguably, caused the most difficulty for the police in the past few decades. The murder of Stephen Lawrence, the failure to bring his killers to justice and the subsequent Macpherson Inquiry received national and international attention, and influenced debate well beyond that simply relating to policing. The Stephen Lawrence Inquiry introduced the concept of 'institutional racism' and the debate over this concept and the other recommendations of the Inquiry continue to dominate policing today, ten years later. This chapter will discuss the Lawrence Inquiry and its implications. It will also discuss some of the earlier police history in dealing with race and racism as well as identifying good present practice. The challenges for the police in dealing with race and racism are best put in the context of the wider criminal justice system, and this is also covered in this chapter. The chapter pays particular attention to hate crime.

Policy and legislation

The most significant legislation relating to racial discrimination was the Race Relations Act 1976, which has now been amended by the Race Relations (Amendment) Act 2000. This Act makes it unlawful to discriminate against anyone on the grounds of race, colour, nationality or ethnic or national origin. Public bodies, including the police and prison services, have a general duty to promote equality of opportunity and it is unlawful for them to discriminate in exercising any of their functions. Public bodies are required to promote racial equality in jobs, training, housing, education and the provision of goods and services. They are required to monitor their workforce and also the impact of their policies and procedures on race equality (Clements and Jones, 2006).

The Crime and Disorder Act 1998 recognised the seriousness of racist crime by establishing a series of new racially aggravated offences. The definition of racist aggravation has provided the template for determining hate crime with regard to the other strands of diversity, so it is worth quoting it in full. According to the Act, offences become racially aggravated if:

> at the time of committing the offence, or immediately before or after doing so, the offender demonstrates towards the victim of the offence hostility based on the victim's membership (or presumed membership) of a racial group; or the offence is motivated (wholly or partly) by hostility towards members of a racial group based on the membership of that group.

'Racial group' was defined by the Act as relating to race, colour, nationality or national origins and, as discussed in the next chapter, presented some difficulties with regard to religious groups by including some, such as Sikhs and Jews, but excluding others, such as Muslims and Catholics. The definition has now been extended to religious groups by the Anti-Terrorism, Crime and Security Act 2001 (Chakraborti and Garland, 2009).

Criminological and sociological perspectives

Race, ethnicity, racism and language

The issue of language is a particularly difficult one in relation to race and ethnicity, and the seeming impossibility of finding a definitive acceptable approach could lead to despair or a decision to stop trying. This is not an option for police officers, who must find accurate and acceptable language. This is also the case for members of the judiciary and useful advice is provided by the Judicial Studies Board (JSB, 2008). It suggests a distinction between *race*, which is used to describe physical, non-changeable characteristics that affect how someone is perceived; *ethnicity*, which defines factors with limited possibility for change, such as nationality and religion; and *culture*, which is determined by factors that are changeable but have a strong association with upbringing, religion and nationality. The JSB (2008) provides specific advice about the use of some terms.

- *Black* is now considered a positive term that can be used descriptively with reference to people of African or Caribbean descent, or politically to refer to all ethnic minority groups.

- The terms *coloured* or *people of colour* should be avoided.

- The terms *minority ethnic*, *minority cultural*, *minority faith*, *multi-cultural* and *multi-faith* are all now considered acceptable.

- The term *British* should be used inclusively and not just to refer to white people, English people or people who follow the Christian religion.

- The terms *immigrants*, *refugees* and *asylum seekers* should be used selectively, carefully and specifically.

- *African-Caribbean* is acceptable but *Afro-Caribbean* and *West Indian* are not. *African* is also acceptable. However, most people will describe themselves in terms of the actual country they come from, including young people born in Britain, who will use the term *black* to describe themselves when they need to do so.

- Similarly, the term *Asian* should be used with care as most people prefer to use a term related to the country or region they come from. It is also not usually used with any accuracy as it is only related to people from southern Asia. *Oriental* is considered an offensive term and should be avoided.

- *Mixed parentage* and *dual heritage* are more acceptable terms than *mixed race*, which is sometimes problematic. *Half-caste* is unacceptable.

REFLECTIVE TASK

Terminology and language

- *Is there anything in the section above that you disagree with or are still confused about? How does that make you feel?*

- *Is it realistic to expect that you might one day have 'all the answers' about the correct terminology to use, or will it always be a process of listening, learning and checking out?*

- *To whom or where will you go for advice regarding some of the difficult decisions?*

Black people as victims and offenders

Criminology has been interested in race and ethnicity since its early origins, but Newburn (2007) suggests an approach that, rather than immediately focusing on black people as offenders, starts by considering their experiences as victims. This section will consider victimisation, and then move on to discuss black people as offenders and racial bias in the wider criminal justice system.

The British Crime Survey was first able to produce data on the victimisation of people from ethnic minorities in 1988 and since then has identified some notable trends (Newburn, 2007) (hate crime is discussed separately later in the chapter).

- People from Asian backgrounds are slightly more likely to be at risk of victimisation, across all categories.

- In general, the risks faced by white people and people from ethnic minorities are about equal.

- People of mixed ethnic origin are at a high risk of victimisation.

- The risks vary depending on types of crime, with one of the most striking discrepancies being that black people are six times more likely to be victims of homicide than white people.

- With regard to fear of crime, people from ethnic minorities are more fearful than white people.

Webster argues:

> *Generally speaking, minority ethnic groups are disproportionately victimised, in part because of where they live – in poorer urban areas – and partly because they tend to be a younger population. They may also suffer from less police concern and protection.*
> (2007, p199)

He goes on to suggest that the same reasons might account for the fact that some people from ethnic minority populations are over-represented with regard to some offending.

Newburn (2007) identifies that, during the 1970s and 1980s, there was a growing trend to consider that offences committed by black people and those committed by white people were different, and that young black men should be feared. He analyses self-report studies showing that white people report the highest level of offending with regard to most offences, with the exception of street robbery, which more black people report having committed than white people. He suggests that this over-representation could be explained by poverty, social exclusion, a desire for status or differences in police decisions made about the definition of offences. White people also reported greater involvement in anti-social behaviour, and patterns of drug use showed that black men and white men had similar drug-taking patterns, with people of mixed ethnic origin reporting much greater use of drugs.

Black people and the wider criminal justice system

Later in this chapter, the police approach and response to black and minority ethnic (BME) people is discussed but, although policing is the focus of this book, it is important to consider also how other aspects of the criminal justice system have treated BME people. This is important, first, because police officers work within a wider criminal justice system context. Second, if the context is neglected it would be easy to make the mistake of assuming that discriminatory behaviour is just a police problem, when in fact there are challenges throughout society in general and the criminal justice system in particular.

Cavadino and Dignan (2007, p351ff) identify points throughout the criminal justice process where bias appears to be present.

- Black people are arrested in numbers disproportionate to their presence in the population.

- Race makes a difference in the decision that the police make whether or not to caution someone.

- Black and Asian defendants are more likely to have prosecutions against them dropped after charge; black defendants are more likely to plead not guilty; and black and Asian defendants who plead not guilty are more likely to be found not guilty. These three pieces of evidence together suggest that the police might charge black and Asian suspects based on a lower level of evidence than that for white suspects.

- Ethnic minority defendants are more likely to be committed for Crown Court trial and, thus, are more likely to attract more severe sentences.

- Black defendants are more likely to be refused bail than white defendants.

- Black people seem to be more likely than white people to receive custodial sentences, although the evidence on that is not entirely consistent.

The Crown Prosecution Service

The CPS took a neutral race blind approach to issues of race and inequality until the Lawrence Inquiry and the subsequent interest that the Commission for Racial Equality (CRE) took in its work (Taylor, 2009). The interest of the CRE caused the CPS to institute its own inquiry into its practice in 2000, known as the Denman Inquiry (CPS, 2001). Taylor (2009) lists its main findings, which included the following.

- One CPS branch, in Croydon, segregated its staff on racial lines. This was addressed in partnership with the CRE.

- BME communities were significantly under-represented in the CPS, particularly at senior levels.

- Training was poor, there was a lack of strategy and there was complacency about the possibility of discrimination.

- The possibility of institutional racism was not considered, and there was variation in practice across areas.

The Inquiry did find some evidence of attempts to address these difficulties and the CPS responded to the Inquiry by significantly improving its practice. The CRE worked with the CPS and, in 2007, commended it for its positive progress, including its engagement with diverse communities in devising policies and monitoring the impact of its practice. Taylor (2009) identifies three areas that the CPS must continue to pay attention to in promoting best diversity practice.

- *Employment*. The CPS has made a lot of positive progress in its employment practice and the racial make-up of its workforce compares favourably to that of the rest of the criminal justice system, including the police, especially at senior levels. The evidence on employee experience, with regard to diversity, is mixed, and there is still some work to do.

- *Prosecutions*. Again, monitoring prosecution decisions in relation to racial equality has only been carried out relatively recently, since 2000. The main concern raised by the early research was that police overcharging often had to be corrected by the CPS. More recently, statistics are continuing to be collated in quite a comprehensive way and are encouraging, particularly in relation to decisions to charge, where there are no significant ethnic differences. There is still a need to monitor practice, however, particularly with regard to decisions to take no further action, and decisions relating to women. Hate crime measurements are already in place.

- *Engaging diverse communities*. The CPS has moved a long way from its initial position that community engagement was not part of its remit. It now has community engagement strategies in place in all areas, and consults diverse communities on matters such as hate crime.

Taylor (2009) argues that, although the CPS was slower to acknowledge diversity issues than some other criminal justice agencies, it has made positive progress and has been able to apply lessons learned in working with racial diversity to other aspects of its practice, such as the prosecution of homophobic crime.

Sentencing and the courts

There has been limited research on how race and ethnicity affects sentencing decisions and the most comprehensive study, in the West Midlands in the 1980s, found that black adult male offenders were slightly more likely to be sent to prison than white adult male offenders, and that there was no evidence of discriminatory practice in how adult female offenders were dealt with (Gelsthorpe, 2006). Newburn (2007) considers two further pieces of research into sentencing decisions that demonstrate differential treatment of people from BME communities. The research carried out in the 1990s found that there was a particular tendency to send more black people to prison for offences of medium seriousness, and that some mitigating factors were less likely to be taken into account if the defendant was black. More recent research shows that there has been some improvement and defendants from ethnic minorities are now much more likely to state that they have been treated in a fair way.

Probation and the National Offender Management Service

The Lawrence Inquiry caused the whole criminal justice system to be subjected to scrutiny with regard to its performance on race and diversity, and the Probation Service was no exception. A report from Her Majesty's Inspectorate of Probation (HMIP) following the Lawrence Inquiry found a decline in the service's commitment to racial equality since the 1970s and 1980s:

> It was disappointing that despite the promise of the work undertaken in the 1980s and early 1990s, so little had been achieved. In many services, understanding of equal opportunities had not progressed beyond the level of treating everyone alike. A number of isolated innovations were found, rather than a corporate approach to race equality. HMIP strongly believes that the promotion of race equality is synonymous with the development of good practice and contributes to the service fulfilling its core task of protecting the public.

(HMIP, 2000, p27)

A follow-up report (HMIP, 2004) found a significant improvement since the initial report, particularly in the way that probation officers treated offenders from ethnic minorities. A further inspection report (HMIP, 2005) found that there was a need for improvement in the practice of dealing with offenders who had committed hate crimes. Interestingly, a Home Office report (2004), seeking the views of black and Asian offenders, found that probation officers were perceived as treating the offenders fairly, but other parts of the criminal justice system, including the police, were perceived as being less fair. Probation officers often had to deal with the consequences of this, as negative experiences of criminal justice affected perceptions of legitimacy, motivation and compliance.

REFLECTIVE TASK

Police and the criminal justice system

Does it surprise you to read that the interaction between a probation officer and the offender he or she is supervising might be affected by how the offender was treated by a police officer many months before? An offender who believes he or she was treated in a racially prejudiced way has difficulty in accepting the legitimacy of any institution in the criminal justice system.

- *Can you think of any other ways in which the practice of an individual police officer might affect, positively or negatively, the work of a colleague elsewhere in the CJS?*

Two main aspects of probation practice are offender assessment and programmes work, and Lewis (2009) considers the diversity aspects of each. The 2000 HMIP report found a significant variation in the proportion of reports that were considered to be of an acceptable standard, with those on white offenders of a higher standard than those on black offenders. National standards gave little guidance on how discrimination could be eliminated. Research in 2004 and 2005 found improvement, but also some continuing cause for concern about reports written on Asian offenders (discussed in the next chapter) and Irish offenders. The use of the Offender Assessment System (OASys) and other standard instruments led to concerns about how well they dealt with diversity issues.

The approach to running probation programmes with minority ethnic offenders was to adapt existing programmes, rather than creating something new. For example, a scenario-based exercise might be located in a shop rather than a pub, to be more culturally sensitive. This approach has attracted criticism for failing to recognise the full differences in the experiences of black and Asian offenders. Lewis (2009) relates further criticism of the Pathfinder project, which was established to measure the effectiveness of pro-grammes, but which revealed little about work with black and Asian offenders.

Lewis (2009) attributes the variable practice with regard to diversity and racial equality in the Probation Service to differences in leadership. He argues that poor leadership led to the disappointing HMIP report in 2000 and expresses concern that the continuing reorganisation and restructuring that has taken place over the last ten years has led to diversity being peripheral rather than central to the National Offender Management Service (NOMS). There is concern that reorganisation into NOMS may involve a move away from the Probation Service's traditions of anti-discrimination and promotion of human rights, which represent such valuable diversity practice.

Prisons

It is clear that black people are over-represented in prisons. As Newburn states, 'The black prison population rate per 1,000 population is over four times higher than that for whites and about seven and a half times that for Asians' (2007, p793). This could be caused by a number of factors, ranging from socio-economics to racism within the criminal justice system. However, as well as this over-representation there is strong evidence to suggest that BME people are treated badly once they are in prison. This treatment can range from verbal and physical abuse and threatening behaviour up to the most serious concerns about deaths in custody. Cavadino and Dignan (2007) describe how stereotypes held by prison officers have led to the best jobs in prisons being allocated to white prisoners. This situation seems to have improved over time and the Prison Service is now committed to the eradication of discrimination.

There is evidence of ethnic differences in the rates of deaths in custody, and there have been some prominent examples over the years of the preventable deaths of black men in custody (Newburn, 2007). The most recent of these examples is that of Zahid Mubarek, who was murdered in his cell by his violent and racist cellmate, Robert Stewart, in Feltham Young Offenders Institution in 2000, while serving a sentence for theft. An official inquiry was ordered into Mubarek's death and it reported in 2006 (Keith, 2006). The report found that the Prison Service was characterised by institutional racism and also suffered from poor systems and poor communication. It found that, at the very least, indications of Stewart's racism were not picked up by prison staff. The report considered the allegation that Stewart and Mubarek had been deliberately put in the same cell to provoke trouble, but the report neither confirmed this nor ruled it out (Bhui, 2009).

Reviews of practice in prisons since Zahid Mubarek's death have continued to raise concerns, with prisoners reporting racist behaviour both from fellow prisoners and from prison staff (Bhui, 2009). This is true for adult men, adult women and juvenile prisoners. The most recent research (HM Inspectorate of Prisons, 2008, summarised in Bhui, 2009) again showed signs of improvement, particularly with regard to leadership and processes, but the outcomes reported by prisoners continued to raise concerns. BME prison staff experienced racism from prisoners, but a much greater emotional effect was caused by the racism from colleagues, often disguised as humour (Bhui, 2009).

The Prison Service has responded to these criticisms and has instigated the decency agenda (discussed in Chapter 1, pages 19–20). Bhui (2009) identifies five main challenges that the Prison Service must face in achieving best diversity practice.

- *Culture change* is very difficult to achieve in any organisation, but particularly in prisons, where the dominant concern is always security. The fact that the prison population is at full capacity also makes it very difficult to focus on the work needed to promote decency and diversity.

- *Prisoner perceptions*: it is important to acknowledge that the previous experience of racism of many prisoners means that any slight difference in treatment by prison staff, even if not motivated by discrimination, can be perceived as racist.

- *Training* for prison officers is very brief – only eight weeks – and does not provide opportunity to reflect on issues of race and diversity.

- A *diverse staff* group is an important objective to try to achieve, not least because it contributes to legitimacy, but it will not in itself be enough to eliminate discrimination.

- *Private prisons* present different difficulties as they are not under the same degree of central control, and have a higher staff turnover.

REFLECTIVE TASK

Bias in the CJS

Cavadino and Dignan (2007, p355) summarise the situation in this way:

> *To sum up: it may not be true to say that there is bias working consistently against black people throughout the entire criminal justice system. Nevertheless, it seems that a black person who comes into contact with the criminal justice system has a good chance of being seriously disadvantaged compared with a white person, and may be particularly likely to end up in prison.*

- *Do you agree with this statement?*

- *What do you think needs to happen to ensure that this statement can no longer be made in, say, ten years' time?*

We have seen in this section that the police response to diversity must be put in the context of the wider criminal justice system. Other agencies have faced similar challenges to those faced by the police, and there are opportunities for learning to be shared between the agencies. The rest of this chapter will focus on the police.

Historical and current police practice

In this section there will be a discussion of the historical and policy context relating to race and policing. However, rather than simply providing a strictly chronological account of this history, the section will highlight key reports (Scarman and Macpherson), significant incidents (the *Secret Policeman* documentary) and contentious policies such as stop and search. In a similar way to the other chapters it will also consider staff relations within the police, as well as the police's role in the community. This section will conclude with a consideration of hate crime.

The Scarman Report

Arguably the first time that the difficult relations between the police and members of minority ethnic communities came to national attention was in the urban disorder that took place in the early 1980s, with the highest-profile incidence of this being the riots in Brixton, London. Lord Scarman, a law lord and therefore a senior establishment figure, was appointed to chair the Inquiry into these riots and made a series of findings and recommendations (Scarman, 1981; Joyce, 2006).

- Current training programmes are inadequate and they need to be adapted to include an emphasis on community relations.

- Steps need to be taken to ensure that police services are more representative of the communities they serve.

- Behaviour that is either racially prejudiced or otherwise discriminatory should be a disciplinary offence, usually leading to dismissal.

- Safeguards should be introduced to monitor the proper use of stop and search.

- The priority of police work should be considered to be the maintenance of public tranquillity, rather than simply law enforcement, and community policing should be encouraged to promote this.

The conclusions of the Scarman Report are generally contrasted with those of the Macpherson Report in light of the understanding that Scarman did not accept the existence of institutional racism. However, Rowe (2004) argues that this is simply a misunderstanding of what is said in the Scarman Report. Scarman defines institutional racism in a particularly narrow way, requiring the existence of a deliberate policy, and therefore states that it is not present in the police. He does, however, acknowledge that there might be indirect racial discrimination present, as defined in the Race Relations Act 1976, and the distinction between that and institutional racism is quite a narrow one.

Joyce (2006) goes on to explain why the Scarman Report had such a limited effect on policing.

- *Recruitment*. The police were not successful in recruiting new members from ethnic minority communities, and this can be partly explained by the poor relationships with those communities that made it difficult to attract applicants.

- *Training*. Although changes in training were made, none of these had a significant or long-term effect, and there was no systematic introduction of a particularly demanding anti-racist training regime.

- *Discriminatory use of police powers*. As discussed below, allegations of the misuse of powers, especially stop and search, continued and the Scarman Report has consistently attracted criticism for failing to address adequately the difficulties with the use of stop and search powers (Bowling and Phillips, 2003).

- *Community liaison*. Formal consultations that were introduced had little impact on the actual relationships between the police and the community.

- *Policing methods*. Community police officers were perceived as having low status, so did not command the confidence of the public, and any positive impact that they had was often undermined by the more aggressive policing carried out by other sections of the force.

- *Failure to address police culture*. Although Scarman did recognise the presence of indirect discrimination, his statement that there was no policy that encouraged racism meant that there was no explicit instruction to police management to address the culture of the organisation.

The Stephen Lawrence Inquiry

The Scarman Report dominated discussions of race relations and policing for over a decade until the murder of Stephen Lawrence and the subsequent Macpherson Inquiry (Macpherson, 1999).

In April 1993 in South London, Stephen Lawrence and his friend, Duwayne Brooks, were making their way home when they were subjected to an unprovoked attack by a gang of white youths. Brooks escaped but Lawrence was so severely wounded that he was unable to do so. Two police officers who arrived at the scene did not provide first aid treatment and, although an ambulance did arrive 25 minutes after the attack, Stephen Lawrence died from his injuries (Rowe, 2004).

The police investigation into the murder was a high-profile and controversial one, even before the Macpherson Report was ordered in 1998 and then published in 1999. The names of five white youths who were the main suspects were provided to the police, but these men were not immediately arrested. The CPS was unable to gather enough evidence to bring successful prosecutions against these subjects and a private prosecution brought by the Lawrence family did not succeed, as eye-witness evidence was declared to be inadmissible. The Coroner's Court determined that Stephen Lawrence was murdered in a racially motivated attack, but was not legally permitted to name the suspects. They were, however, named by a national newspaper following the coroner's verdict (Rowe, 2004).

The Conservative government resisted all requests to have a public inquiry into the murder of Stephen Lawrence, but one was ordered by Jack Straw, the then new Home Secretary, immediately after the election of the Labour government in 1997. The Inquiry was chaired by Sir William Macpherson, a retired High Court judge, and took evidence from police officers of all ranks as well as other expert witnesses. The report was published in 1999 (Macpherson, 1999) and Rowe (2004) identifies three main themes.

- *Police incompetence*. The Inquiry identified a series of mistakes that were made, particularly in the early stages of the investigation. These included mistakes by individual officers as well as failings in the use of computer systems. The Lawrence family had a particularly bad experience of the police, from the time of the initial incident, when first aid support was not provided to Stephen, right through the investigation into his murder, where the police behaved insensitively and failed to keep them informed of progress and developments. The report criticised both junior officers for their errors and more senior officers for their failure to provide leadership.

- *Police corruption*. There were rumours of corruption involving the possible threatening of witnesses or bribery of police officers, but Macpherson did not conclude that police corruption had any role in the investigation.

- *Institutional racism*. The Macpherson Report did not invent the term 'institutional racism' but it did introduce it to a wide audience and provided a definition of it that is now widely accepted:

The collective failure of an organisation to provide an appropriate and professional service to people because of their colour, culture or ethnic origin. It can be seen or detected in processes, attitudes and behaviour which amount to discrimination through unwitting prejudice, ignorance, thoughtlessness and racist stereotyping which disadvantages minority ethnic people.

(Macpherson, 1999, para. 6:34)

The Macpherson Inquiry found that the police service was institutionally racist, and this finding has influenced much of what has happened in the police in the last ten years. Institutional racism is an evocative term, and is often used in a way that is unclear, but its definition is not dissimilar to the definition of indirect discrimination in the Race Relations Act 1976, which relates to actions that are not designed to discriminate but have the effect of doing so (Rowe, 2004). Souhami (2007, p67) describes the term as being 'comprehensively misunderstood' within the police, with a continued focus on understanding racism in terms of the actions of individuals.

It is useful to draw a distinction in the reaction to the report between the official response and that from serving officers within the police service (Souhami, 2007). The official response was led by Sir Paul Condon, Commissioner of the Metropolitan Police, and Jack Straw, Home Secretary, and accepted the term institutional racism and its new definition. It was, perhaps, easier for organisations to accept that their institutional processes were racist than to attribute racism to individuals. Serving police officers were more likely to respond with anger to the report, perceiving that it had accused all police constables of being racist individuals. This perception was strengthened by their interaction with the public, as many officers had the experience of being labelled as racists by members of the public in the months following the report.

Police officers, understandably reluctant to accept a charge of racism, were inclined to explain the failings highlighted in the Stephen Lawrence Inquiry as being caused by the incompetence of the investigating officers, rather than by either individual or institutional racism. Officers outside London could also interpret the events as being particular to the Metropolitan Police and thus having little to do with them.

Nearly all of the Lawrence Inquiry's recommendations were accepted by the police and the findings of the Inquiry have changed both the policing climate and the political climate, putting racism at the top of the police agenda (Newburn, 2007). Later in the chapter the actual changes that have taken place in the ten years since the Inquiry will be discussed.

PRACTICAL TASK

Institutional racism

In your own words, define institutional racism and explain how it applied to the Metropolitan Police at the time of the murder of Stephen Lawrence.

How would you recognise it if you saw it? Look again at the definition; are any of the following examples possible instances of institutional racism?

- *Two police constables visit the home of a black couple, Paul and Alison, who have been the victims of a home burglary. As he is being shown around the house, the first constable comments that it is unlikely that the crime would ever be solved, but unfortunately this sort of incident is all too common around here as there is a high immigrant population and immigrants cannot be expected to share British values.*

- *As the police officers are leaving the house, Alison asks the second officer if he shares his colleague's views about immigrants. The second officer says he is just there to do his job, not to discuss politics.*

- *Paul and Alison submit a letter of complaint to the local station, explaining that they were offended by the officer's comments as they are both from immigrant families, and they feel that they have strong values, as do their friends and families. After three weeks have passed they phone the police station to request a progress report on the burglary investigation and a reply to their letter. After checking, the officer who answered the phone says that there is no new information on the burglary, and they have no record of receiving a letter.*

- *After three months have passed without anyone being arrested for the burglary or their goods being recovered, Paul and Alison look into crime detection statistics for their local constabulary and discover that their area has a high level of crime, but the lowest level of detection in the region.*

Stop and search

Elements of the police have had stop and search powers, in one form or another, throughout their history and the use of these powers has long been contentious, particularly in the 1970s (Rowe, 2004). The police powers, which depended a lot on individual discretion, and were therefore vulnerable to being subject to bias and stereotyping (Sanders and Young, 2003), were consolidated by the Police and Criminal Evidence Act (PACE) 1984, which created the threshold of reasonable suspicion:

> *A constable may stop, search and detain an individual if there is reasonable suspicion that they are carrying stolen or prohibited articles.*
>
> (Rowe, 2004, p83)

Two further pieces of legislation since then have given the police stop and search powers: section 60 of the Criminal Justice and Public Order Act 1994, and section 44 of the Terrorism Act 2000 (Newburn, 2007).

PACE also provided for the recording and monitoring of the use of stop and search powers, but this recording was only required to take account of the ethnic origin of the suspects from 1993. Since these records have been kept it has been clear that black people have consistently been stopped more than white people, and in some years have been stopped as much as eight times as often (Rowe, 2004). There is a similar profile to stops under the other legislation, but Newburn cautions against simply interpreting this as being caused by racism, explaining that, if the 'available population' is considered (that is, those people actually on the street), the differences no longer appear (2007, p787). However, this then raises different questions about which streets the police choose to patrol (Rowe, 2004). A related concern is that the police are less likely to speak courteously and respectfully to people from BME communities when they do stop and search them, and this again damages relations and police claims to legitimacy (Sanders and Young, 2003).

There remain concerns about how the powers to strip-search prisoners are used against different ethnic groups, and the combination of all these factors leads to a very important perception among people from minority ethnic communities that they are not treated fairly by the police, and so lack confidence in the work of the police (Newburn, 2007). The Macpherson Report also addressed this issue, stating:

> *We are clear that the perception and experience of the minority communities that discrimination is a major element in the stop and search problem is correct.*
>
> (Macpherson, 1999, para. 45:8)

One of the ways in which the issue of stop and search is important in determining relations between minority ethnic communities and the police is that emotive personal accounts can be reinforced by official statistics to provide a powerful story about police practice (Stenson and Waddington, 2007). Thus, an individual who feels aggrieved at being stopped and searched can, regardless of the details of that particular case, refer to the national statistics on stop and search and interpret his or her own experience as being an example of police racism.

Stop and search

Police officers have considerable discretion in the use of stop and search powers and make decisions quickly, and the circumstances mean that they usually have limited information to go on. Their decisions are usually 'invisible to supervisory officers' (Bowling and Phillips, 2003, p535) and are therefore subject to limited accountability.

Imagine you are a police officer patrolling, by car, a suburban street close to a town centre at 11 p.m. one evening. You see three young men walking towards you on the other side of the road. In what circumstances might you make the decision to stop and search them? How would you respond in the following scenarios?

- *The three men are white, wearing football tops, and appear to be drunk. They are singing loudly and you think you hear one use a racist term.*

- *The three men are black and appear to be sober. You know that the area you are driving through has a mainly white population, and you do not recognise these men as coming from the area.*

- *The group consists of two white men and one Asian man. They are all wearing baseball caps and you see one man hand an item to his companion. You cannot tell what this item is, but it appears to be a small metal object.*

The Secret Policeman

The highest-profile incident since the Lawrence Inquiry relating to race and policing involved an undercover journalist making a BBC documentary called *The Secret Policeman*. The BBC sent reporter Mark Daly undercover to train and then work as a police constable in Greater Manchester Police (GMP), to discover whether racism in the police had been eradicated or simply driven underground. He recorded conversations with police officers in classrooms, social settings and private settings, such as his car or his bedroom. In these conversations a number of officers showed a hatred of Asians, an inclination to discriminate as operational officers and sympathy for far-right political groups (McLaughlin, 2007).

The broadcasting of the programme led to a strong and immediate response from the police and from the Home Office. The internal investigations led to the resignation of ten officers and the disciplining of twelve others. Assistant Chief Constables of both GMP and North Wales condemned the racist officers. ACPO agreed to work with the Black Police Association (BPA), the CRE (since incorporated into the EHRC) and other groups to review all aspects of professional development, training and recruitment practice. Trevor Phillips was then chair of the CRE and he emphasised that it was important not simply to dismiss what was discovered as being evidence of a few 'rotten apples', but to concentrate on what it was about police culture that made these officers think that it was acceptable to express these views without fear of the consequences. He said that what was required was not simply more diversity training, but deep organisational transformation (McLaughlin, 2007).

Holland (2007, p177) described *The Secret Policeman* as a 'catalyst for change' in GMP that led to the formulation of the Respect Programme. It built on work that had already been done following the Lawrence Inquiry, but added an element of individual responsibility and personal commitment, using language designed to engage both front-line police officers and more senior staff.

Following *The Secret Policeman*, reviews into the employment practices of the police found that there were still problems with the recruitment and retention of ethnic minority police constables. This was less true of PCSOs, but BME staff remain significantly under-represented at management grades. Newburn puts together the information on employment, victimisation and offending to summarise, thus:

> *Under-representation in criminal justice professions – particularly at senior levels – and over-representation as suspects, arrestees, defendants and among those serving sentences in prisons and in the community, perhaps captures the central problem confronting us when considering the area of ethnicity and criminal justice.*
>
> (2007, p801)

Notwithstanding the positive steps that have been taken to address the problems identified in *The Secret Policeman*, the programme has been hugely damaging. The police have long had the reputation, fairly or unfairly, of basing decisions that they make on racial stereotyping rather than evidence (Bowling and Phillips, 2003) and the documentary appeared to prove that this continued to be the case for some officers. The evidence uncovered in the documentary is regularly used to argue against giving the police greater discretion in stop and search powers or in prosecuting hate crime (see, for example, Hall, 2005). The damage to the police's reputation was caused not just by the actions of the individual officers, but by the failure of their police colleagues to respond appropriately.

REFLECTIVE TASK

Grassing

As discussed above, one of the concerns expressed by Trevor Phillips about the behaviour recorded in The Secret Policeman, was that police officers who expressed racist views felt free to do so in front of their colleagues. It is easy to condemn those who did not report the comments and behaviour, but in reality it is often very difficult to report concerns. Being accused of being a 'grass' is a term of abuse and those who report the behaviour of colleagues are considered to be disloyal and untrustworthy. This is a particularly damaging accusation in an organisation such as the police, where staff are very dependent on the support of colleagues.

Consider the following examples and ask yourself whether you would do nothing, challenge the individuals concerned directly, or report them to a higher authority.

- *You are in class being taught a practical session by a white, male police inspector. He spots a book on diversity on your desk and says 'All this nonsense about diversity has gone too far. Soon only black lesbians will be able to achieve promotion in the police.'*

- *You go for a drink after class with some friends, one of whom is a trainee police constable. After a few drinks he starts expounding, at length, his view that it is perfectly legitimate for the police to be suspicious of all 'young Asian-looking men', as that is the group that terrorists are likely to come from. During this conversation another police trainee joins in, supporting this view and using an offensive term to describe Asian men.*

- *A police trainer is delivering a session on homophobia. She introduces the session by saying that she is delivering this because it is on the curriculum, and she does not think it is right that anyone should be discriminated against, bullied or assaulted. However, she goes on to say that she personally holds strong religious views and believes that homosexuality is sinful and that marriage should be between a man and a woman.*

Police staff: recruitment and retention

The fact that it is only recently that the police have given attention to matters of race and diversity is illustrated by considering the make-up of the police. As recently as the 1960s there were no black and Asian police officers employed in the UK (Bowling and Phillips, 2003). Although there were improvements in the next few decades, BME communities remained significantly under-represented, and one of the recommendations of the Macpherson Report was that the police should take steps to increase their recruitment of BME officers (Rowe, 2009). Targets were set, with the objective of ensuring that the make-up of the police reflected the make-up of the society that they served, and a lot of effort and energy has gone into public relations and recruitment campaigns aimed at BME communities. The progress in recruiting police officers has been slow, although it is moving in a positive direction. The police have had much more success in recruiting BME candidates to other roles: special constables and PCSOs are much more diverse in ethnic origin than police officers (Rowe, 2009).

HMIC investigated the police employment culture, following *The Secret Policeman*. This report was never published, but the EHRC refers to it in a later report (EHRC, 2009). One particular concern expressed in the HMIC report was the difficulty that BME officers found in gaining access to specialist units, such as firearms or anti-terrorist squads.

Although aiming to create a police service that is as diverse as the wider community is a positive objective, care needs to be taken in achieving this. First, attracting police officers from a particular community, with the explicit aim of better addressing crime associated with that community, could put such officers at risk. Second, it is tempting, but erroneous, to assume that someone from a particular community somehow 'represents' that community, and this can obscure the diversity that is found within communities.

Hate crime

In other chapters, it has been discussed how hate crime is a relatively new phenomenon and has only recently come to the attention of the criminal justice system. This is much less the case in relation to racist hate crime, and British history shows that immigrant communities, including those of Jewish and Irish immigrants, have long been treated with suspicion and hostility, with racism being particularly common and hostile in the three decades following the Second World War (Hall, 2005). Considering the history of hate crime demonstrates that there are strong similarities between hate crime in the past and modern hate crime in the characteristics of the offenders, the victims and the offences themselves (Hall, 2005).

An important year in the history of hate crime in the UK was 1981. In that year, there were inner-city riots and a fire at New Cross station in which 13 black people died in what was possibly a racially motivated attack. That year was also the first year that violence targeted at an ethnic minority community was officially noted by the Home Office (Newburn, 2007). However, as with much else discussed in this chapter, it was the Lawrence Inquiry that brought a lot of attention to racist hate crimes. The Labour government disagreed with the view of the previous Conservative administration – that all crime could be dealt with under existing laws and there was no need for additional legislation – and enacted the Crime and Disorder Act 1998, discussed at the beginning of the chapter. The other significant change following the Lawrence Inquiry was that the Macpherson Report's definition of a racist incident gained widespread acceptance:

A racist incident is any incident which is perceived to be racist by the victim or any other person.

(Macpherson, 1999, 47:12)

This is a subjective definition that emphasises the experience of the victim, in contrast to the previous definition, which required a police officer to make a judgement. The combination of this new definition, the high profile given to racially motivated crime and, perhaps, the increased confidence in the police led to a significant increase in the amount of racist crime reported to the police in the years following the Lawrence Inquiry. This will be discussed in the next section, which considers the police's response to racial diversity, including hate crime, in the decade since the Lawrence Inquiry.

Best current police practice and plans for the future

The Stephen Lawrence Inquiry – ten years on

The tenth anniversary, in 2009, of the Stephen Lawrence Inquiry led to a series of reports and reviews of the progress that had been made. This reflection was not solely about policing; the Macpherson findings affected every aspect of society, so the tenth anniversary was an opportunity for society as a whole to reflect. In this section, four of the reports that looked at policing will be considered.

The National Black Police Association

The National Black Police Association (NBPA) (discussed below) surveyed its 43 areas to establish how black police officers felt that the Lawrence recommendations had been met. The main findings of this research include the following (NBPA, 2009).

- Trust in the police force remains a problem, both from community members and from BME officers.

- The definition of institutional racism in the Macpherson Report is a helpful one that has been instrumental in effecting change.

- The implementation of change is inconsistent between areas.

- Many black officers still experience stereotypical assumptions being made about them because of their colour, including that they might be lazy, unpatriotic or dishonest.

- Black staff are concerned about the use of stop and search procedures.

- Some forces will discuss the diversity agenda without addressing the really difficult issues, or will use diversity training simply as a way of avoiding liability at a tribunal.

The Equality and Human Rights Commission

The EHRC report considered the progress that the police had made since the Lawrence Inquiry against four main themes (EHRC, 2009).

- *Employment, training, retention and promotion*. Although the EHRC acknowledged that senior police leaders wanted recruitment and retention targets to be met, it expressed disappointment at the slow progress made. *The Secret Policeman* revealed the nature of police occupational culture and black officers continued to be significantly under-represented in specialist squads.

- *Stop and search*. The Commission expressed concern that the use of stop and search powers continued to have a disproportionate impact on the black community and that there had been no real change in this in 20 years.

- *The national DNA database*. Black men are four times more likely than white men to have their details stored on the DNA database, and the EHRC continues to investigate whether the government is complying with its racial equality duties in relation to the database.

- *Race hate crimes*. The EHRC was pleased with the progress that the police had made in this area, and the improvement both in process and in recording.

House of Commons Home Affairs Select Committee

The House of Commons Home Affairs Select Committee (HoC, 2009) also used the ten-year anniversary as an opportunity to assess the progress that had been made. The committee was informed by the EHRC and also took evidence, including from Doreen Lawrence, coming up with a series of conclusions and recommendations. The Committee was impressed with the progress that the police had made and the leadership that had been shown. However, it expressed concern about the continued over-representation of black people in the criminal justice system, and particularly their continued over-representation in police stop and search statistics, particularly as this now leads to inclusion on the national DNA database. The Committee also expressed disappointment that there continued to be discrimination within the service and that the police had not met the employment targets set following the Macpherson Report.

Runnymede Trust

The Runnymede Trust produced an extensive review of the literature (Rollock, 2009) to analyse progress in meeting the Macpherson expectations. Their report made five key recommendations.

- There should be sharing across the criminal justice system of effective practice in recording racist incidents.

- There needs to be an improvement in how the police monitor racially motivated crime.

- The publication of a Public Inquiry Report should mark the start of a period of scrutiny, not the end of it.

- The problems in the progression and retention of BME staff must be addressed by all police forces.

- The effectiveness of stop and search as a crime control policy must be reviewed by the government.

Overall messages from the reports

Before considering the main themes to come from the reports, it is worth noting the way that the tenth anniversary was reported by the media, as that provides insight into the highly charged context in which the police must work with diversity. *The Guardian*, a traditionally left-wing paper, ran a number of articles, including an interview with Doreen Lawrence, Stephen's mother, and a column crediting Sir William Macpherson with many of the positive changes, with regard to diversity, that have happened in society in the past decade (Muir, 2009).

The *Daily Mail*, a traditionally right-wing paper, and one that had received a lot of praise for its reporting of the Lawrence murder, including its publication of names and photographs of the main suspects, took a different approach. It focused on the suggestion that employment diversity targets, set following the Macpherson Report, made it more difficult for white men to get jobs. The paper reported, with approval, that these targets were to be scrapped. It revisited a story from 2006, when Gloucestershire Police Service had deselected over 100 white recruits in an attempt at positive discrimination that it later admitted was unlawful (Slack, 2009). A brief consideration of these varying media reports indicates that the police must approach diversity practice in the knowledge that all they do is subject to scrutiny and that, if they respond too slowly, they are likely to face criticism from some sections of the media or society, but if they are deemed to go too far in the other direction they will face criticism from others.

The reports discussed above contained some original research, as well as the views of people and organisations who know the police well and have a lot of experience in diversity issues. Drawing the reports and responses together gives a clear and comprehensive picture of how the police have responded in the ten years since the Macpherson Report.

All agreed that there had been improvement in police practice and the most commonly acknowledged examples of this included the response to hate crime and the commitment of police leaders to address previous failings. The discussion of institutional racism in the Macpherson Report, and the way in which the term was defined, was considered to be helpful. However, there were also some very strong messages about continuing concerns. Black people continue to be over-represented as offenders in the criminal justice system, and there remains mistrust between the black community and the police. Stop and search policy, and its impact on different sections of the community, has been a long-standing source of controversy and this continues to be the case. The introduction of the national DNA database has brought another dimension of concern to this. In the decade since the Lawrence Inquiry, the police have also had limited success in the recruitment, retention and promotion of black staff, and staffing issues will now be considered in the following section.

REFLECTIVE TASK

The Lawrence Inquiry – ten years on

If you could suggest one simple, practical measure or improvement that the police could make to continue their progress since the Lawrence Inquiry, and to address the ongoing concerns, what would it be?

Police staff

The National Black Police Association

A Black Police Association was first formed in the Metropolitan Police in 1994 to support and advise black staff in the police. Prior to its formation, black staff in the police were reluctant to speak to, or even acknowledge, each other, given the prevailing culture in the organisation (Rowe, 2004). This association did communicate with groups throughout the country, but the stimulus for the creation of a national organisation really came about because of the Macpherson Report. The NBPA was given new status, and funding, by the Report and by Home Secretary Jack Straw's response to it (Holdaway and O'Neill, 2007). This status gave them a voice in discussions about both policy and practice, and made it politically difficult for any constabulary to be seen to be ignoring their advice. However, as Rowe (2004) points out, the support of senior officers does not necessarily prevent more junior staff from frustrating the work of the NBPA.

The NBPA website expresses its vision:

> *The NBPA will work in the interests of the UK police services and be an integral partner to ensure equitable service for all and for the Black and Minority Ethnic (BME) staff who we represent.*

We will also advocate the needs and expectations of BME communities by delivering and supporting strategies and initiatives which have a positive impact on all.

Interestingly, the NBPA declares that its definition of 'black' does not relate to skin colour, but that it emphasises the common experience of those who have origins in Africa, Asia or the Caribbean. This is consistent with Holdaway and O'Neill's (2007) observation that the NBPA has been effective in drawing people together, but has found it challenging to settle on a definition of race and ethnicity that is both meaningful and inclusive. Some local associations prefer the term 'black and Asian' and, as discussed in the next chapter, there have also been separate associations formed to represent police staff from particular religious groups.

The wider police family

As mentioned above, despite the difficulties that the police have had in recruiting BME officers, they have achieved greater success in recruiting a diverse workforce to the wider police family. Special constables, of which there are 14,000 in England and Wales, continue to play an important role in policing and are a significant part of the government's plans to reform policing practice and make the police more visible (Jones, 2009). Even more significantly, PCSOs have an increasingly crucial role to play. They have limited powers but are encouraged to be visible in the community and to interact with the public, including young people. The initial popularity of PCSOs led to the government announcing that there would be an increase in their number, to 24,000 in 2008 (Bryant et al., 2006). As PCSOs become more established within the police family, their powers are being extended and, in many constabularies, they are also receiving training of increasing quality and duration.

Many PCSOs join the police service with the explicit aim of eventually becoming police officers, and some take PCSO posts as a way of trying the job out, to see if they like it. This is particularly true of those from BME communities who wish to establish how they will be treated (Rowe, 2009). As has already been discussed, the PCSO workforce is a more diverse one than the police constable workforce. Thus, as they become more established, with greater powers and training, and clearer pathways into the police constable role, that can only increase the diversity of the whole police workforce.

REFLECTIVE TASK

Positive discrimination

Positive discrimination is illegal, and Gloucestershire Police Service had to apologise for its policy and change its recruitment practice. However, all other attempts to increase the diversity among police constables have been less than completely successful.

- *In your view, is increasing the profile and responsibilities of auxiliary police officers the right approach? Or should the police take the more radical approach of seeking a change in employment law to allow them to practise positive discrimination? (As will*

REFLECTIVE TASK *continued*

be discussed in the next chapter, the second approach is the one that has been taken by the Police Service of Northern Ireland (PSNI)).

*   *Are white men right to be concerned about their prospects of advancement in the modern police?*

Hate crime

As racist hate crime is more established than hate crime against other groups, there has also been more research into the people who commit such crimes. Research shows that prejudice on its own is not sufficient motivation for the commission of hate crime; that such offenders usually come from socially and economically deprived areas; and that hate crime is committed by young men with:

> *Deep-seated feelings of alienation, shame and rage characteristic of males trapped in deprived and run-down estates with little positive contact with people of different ethnic origins.*

(Newburn, 2007, p779)

Hall (2005) summarises research that found that offenders who committed hate crime belonged to one of four categories.

*   Thrill seekers, who committed racist offences out of boredom or the need for excitement.

*   Defensive offenders, who believed that people from minority ethnic communities had moved into their area and were in some way threatening it, and that their offending was simply defending their territory.

*   Retaliatory offenders, who committed racist offences for revenge. These revenge attacks were most evident following 9/11, when there was a sharp increase in attacks on Muslims.

*   'Mission' offenders, who were absolutely committed to their prejudiced views and were often members of race hate groups.

REFLECTIVE TASK

Racially motivated offenders

If the description of the profile of racially motivated offenders above is correct, and most racially aggravated offending is committed by bored young men from socially deprived areas, what steps could be taken to address such offending? What role might it be possible for the police to play?

Studying the victims of hate crime is much more complicated, as they come from a variety of backgrounds and communities. There is always a risk of generalising too widely and failing to take account of the experiences of some victims. For example, those people who come from a mixed heritage background have a very particular experience, and gypsies and travellers can often be excluded from accounts of racist hate crime, even though gypsies are now recognised by the law as a distinct ethnic group (Chakraborti and Garland, 2009).

The police have considerable discretion in determining whether a particular incident should be prosecuted as a hate crime and research has been carried out in the USA to investigate how that discretion is used. It was found that the police were likely to take into account the nature of the incident, the identities of both offender and victim, the credibility of the victim, whether racist language was used, and the age of the offender, with young offenders being very unlikely to be prosecuted for hate crime (Bell, 2002). This demonstrates the need for police officers to have an understanding of hate crime that goes beyond just knowledge of the law, and demonstrates true insight into the characteristics of offenders and their impact on victims.

The police have faced difficulties and challenges with the law on racial aggravation since its introduction. The Crime and Disorder Act 1998 has created expectations that are difficult to fulfil, as in reality defendants will often 'plea bargain' away the racist element of the offence, pleading guilty to the main charge so that the racist aggravation element is removed. There is also a risk that the term 'hostility' in the legislation and the even wider definition of a racist incident used by the police (discussed below) can be defined extremely generously. This has two negative effects: first, in drawing in those who were never intended to be included in the ambit of the offence; and, second, in provoking a sense of injustice and unfair treatment that can often be a precipitating or aggravating factor in racist offending (Chakraborti and Garland, 2009).

As discussed earlier, the reviews of police practice since the Macpherson Report have been positive about the advances that the police have made in tackling hate crime. The EHRC identified what it considered were the two main factors in this positive progress:

> *The Commission believes that initiatives such as Multi-Agency Panels, reporting networks and the Association of Chief Police Officers' Hate Crime Guide have all contributed to the improvements made in reducing racist incidents over the past decade.*
>
> (2009, p7)

The police did take a multi-agency approach to hate crime before the Macpherson Report, but this was done inconsistently and some panels existed in name only. This practice has significantly improved in the decade since Macpherson, and the multi-agency approach has led to a greater number of cases being dealt with by the right agency, as well as an increase in the confidence in reporting expressed by members of the public. For example, Coventry City Council publicises on its website that hate crime can be reported at many community venues, including housing and council offices. These complaints are then investigated by the Coventry Anti-Harassment Forum, which is made up of agencies including the police, the Council, Victim Support and housing associations (Coventry City

Council, 2009). The Forum does not simply focus on prosecuting offenders, but also supports victims and seeks to prevent further instances.

The main contribution that the ACPO guides (2000, 2005) have made to the hate crime debate has been in establishing the definition of hate crime and therefore setting the agenda both for academic debate and for police practice. The definition is a broad one, allowing anyone to be a victim of a hate crime, and including offences motivated by prejudice as well as hate. However, this broad police policy definition is slightly at odds with the legal definition, which sets tighter boundaries around what is considered to be hate crime (Hall, 2005).

The guidance also distinguishes between hate crime and hate incidents. The definition of hate incidents includes hate crimes, but the definition is wider and in line with Macpherson, in that it requires anything perceived by the victim as a hate incident to be recorded as such, even though it may not constitute a crime. It is consistent with Macpherson that the determination of whether something constitutes a hate incident is based on the subjective experience of the victim, rather than the discretion of the police officer (Chakraborti and Garland, 2009).

Good police practice

The two aspects of police practice praised by the EHRC as contributing to the reduction in racist incidents are multi-agency work and adherence to the ACPO guidelines. These have in common that they take the police away from 'traditional' police work (that is, investigating crime and arresting offenders) into newer roles of crime prevention, victim support and the recording of incidents that are not strictly offences.

- *How do you feel about that?*

- *If you are a police officer or aspire to be a police officer, is this the sort of work that you would be interested in doing, and do you think it is suitable for the police?*

C H A P T E R   S U M M A R Y

As we have seen in this chapter, race is probably the most contentious diversity issue in society and is an extremely difficult one to resolve within the criminal justice system. Legal changes are made, but these on their own are not enough, as they require interpretation and implementation. When criminal justice institutions fail in this regard the consequences are extremely serious for individual victims and their families. However, the fact that the names of Stephen Lawrence and Zahid Mubarek are widely known, and that the implications of Scarman, Macpherson and *The Secret Policeman* have been felt well beyond the police, shows that the actions of police officers, and other criminal justice workers, have an impact on the whole of society.

Discussing the history of race and policing can sometimes feel like relating a litany of controversy, shame and failure, but the 2009 reports into the decade since Macpherson do provide some grounds for optimism in the positive progress that is being made in dealing with hate crime and the leadership that is being shown by senior officers.

REFERENCES

Association of Chief Police Officers (ACPO) (2000) *Guide to Identifying and Combating Hate Crime*. London: ACPO.

Association of Chief Police Officers (ACPO) (2005) *Hate Crime: Delivering a Quality Service – Good Practice and Tactical Guidance*. London: Home Office Police Standards Unit.

Bell, J (2002) *Policing Hatred: Law Enforcement, Civil Rights and Hate Crime*. New York and London: New York University Press.

Bhui, H (2009) Prisons and race equality, in Bhui, HS (ed.) *Race and Criminal Justice*. London: Sage.

Bowling, B and Phillips, C (2003) Policing minority ethnic communities, in Newburn, T (ed.) *Handbook of Policing*. Cullompton: Willan.

Bryant, R, Caless, B, Lawton-Barrett, K, Underwood, R and Wood, D (2006) *Blackstone's Student Police Officer Handbook*. Oxford: Oxford University Press.

Cavadino, M and Dignan, J (2007) *The Penal System: An Introduction*, 4th edition. London: Sage.

Chakraborti, N and Garland, J (2009) *Hate Crime: Impact, Causes and Responses*. London: Sage.

Clements, P and Jones, J (2006) *The Diversity Training Handbook*. London: Kogan Page.

Coventry City Council (2009) *Hate Crime*. Available online at www.coventry.gov.uk/ccm/safety/hate-crime.en.jsessionid=bRpqJfdCTbG6 (accessed 15 August 2009).

Crown Prosecution Service (2001) *Report of an Independent Inquiry into Race Discrimination in the Crown Prosecution Service* (Denman Report). London: CPS.

Equality and Human Rights Commission (EHRC) (2009) *Police and Racism: What Has Been Achieved 10 Years after the Stephen Lawrence Inquiry Report*. Available online at www.equalityhumanrights.com/uploaded_files/raceinbritain/policeandracism.pdf (accessed 15 March 2010).

Gelsthorpe, L (2006) The experiences of female minority ethnic offenders: the other 'other', in Lewis, S, Raynor, P, Smith D and Wardak, A (eds) *Race and Probation*. Cullompton: Willan.

Hall, N (2005) *Hate Crime*. Cullompton: Willan.

HM Inspectorate of Prisons (2008) *Annual Report*. London: Ministry of Justice.

HM Inspectorate of Probation (HMIP) (2000) *Towards Race Equality*, London: Home Office.

HM Inspectorate of Probation (HMIP) (2004) *Towards Race Equality – Follow-up Inspection Report*. London: Home Office.

HM Inspectorate of Probation (HMIP) (2005) *'I'm not a racist but . . .': An Inspection of National Probation Service Work with Racially Motivated Offenders*. London: Home Office.

Holdaway, S and O'Neill, M (2007) Black police associations and the Lawrence Report, in Rowe, M (ed.) *Policing Beyond Macpherson: Issues in Policing, Race and Society*. Cullompton: Willan.

Holland, B (2007) View from within: the realities of promoting race and diversity inside the police service, in Rowe, M (ed.) *Policing Beyond Macpherson: Issues in Policing, Race and Society*. Cullompton: Willan.

Home Office (2004) *Black and Asian Offenders on Probation: Home Office Research Study 277*. London: Home Office Research, Development and Statistics Directorate.

House of Commons Home Affairs Select Committee (HoC) (2009) *The Macpherson Report – Ten Years On*. Available online at www.parliament.the-stationery-office.co.uk/pa/cm200809/cmselect/cmhaff/427/42703.htm (accessed 15 August 2009).

Jones, T (2009) Auxiliary police, in Wakefield, A and Fleming, J (eds) *The Sage Dictionary of Policing*. London: Sage.

Joyce, P (2006) *Criminal Justice*. Cullompton: Willan.

Judicial Studies Board (JSB) (2008) *Equal Treatment Bench Book: 1.1: Equality and Justice*. Available online at www.jsboard.co.uk/etac/downloads/equality_and_justice.doc (accessed 15 March 2010).

Keith, B (2006) *Report of the Zahid Mubarek Inquiry, Volumes 1 and 2*. London: The Stationery Office.

Lewis, S (2009) The Probation Service and race equality, in Bhui, H (ed.) *Race and Criminal Justice*. London: Sage.

Macpherson, Sir W (1999) *The Stephen Lawrence Inquiry*. London: HMSO.

McLaughlin, E (2007) Diversity or anarchy? The post-Macpherson blues, in Rowe, M (ed.) *Policing Beyond Macpherson: Issues in Policing, Race and Society*. Cullompton: Willan.

Muir, H (2009) Macpherson's rules of engagement, *The Guardian*, 23 February.

Newburn, T (2007) *Criminology*. Cullompton: Willan.

National Black Police Association (NBPA) (2009) *The Post Stephen Lawrence Decade*. Available online at www.nbpa.co.uk/images/NBPA_Reports/post_stephen_lawrence_nbpa_review_2009.pdf

Rollock, N. (2009) *The Stephen Lawrence Inquiry 10 Years On – An Analysis of the Literature*. London: Runnymede Trust.

Rowe, M (2004) *Policing, Race and Racism* Cullompton: Willan.

Rowe, M (2009) Policing and race equality: thinking outside the (tick) box, in Bhui, H (ed.) *Race and Criminal Justice*. London: Sage.

Sanders, A and Young, R (2003) Police powers, in Newburn, T (ed.) *Handbook of Policing*. Cullompton: Willan.

Scarman, Lord (1981) *The Brixton Disorders: 10–12 April 1981 – Report of an Inquiry by the Rt Hon Lord Scarman, OBE*. London: HMSO.

Slack, J (2009) Ten years after Macpherson, police race quotas are axed, *Daily Mail*, 20 February.

Souhami, A (2007) Understanding institutional racism: the Stephen Lawrence Inquiry and the police service reaction, in Rowe, M (ed.) *Policing Beyond Macpherson: Issues in Policing, Race and Society*. Cullompton: Willan.

Stenson, K. and Waddington, P A J (2007) Macpherson, police stops and institutionalised racism, in Rowe, M (ed.) *Policing Beyond Macpherson: Issues in Policing, Race and Society*. Cullompton: Willan.

Taylor, S (2009) The Crown Prosecution Service and race equality, in Bhui, H (ed.) *Race and Criminal Justice*. London: Sage.

Webster, Colin (2007) *Understanding Race and Crime*. Maidenhead: Open University Press.

FURTHER READING

Policing Beyond Macpherson, edited by Michael Rowe (2007), effectively puts the Macpherson recommendations into the context of current police practice. In particular, 'institutional racism' remains a difficult concept to understand properly and Anna Souhami's chapter in Rowe's book provides a very helpful discussion of how the term was explained by Macpherson and how it has subsequently been understood. The four reports discussed above, which were produced to mark the tenth anniversary of the Macpherson Report, are well worth reading in their entirety.

USEFUL WEBSITES

www.coventry.gov.uk/ccm/safety/hate-crime.en;jsessionid=bRpqJfdCTbG6 (Coventry City Council's information on hate crime)

www.jsboard.co.uk/etac/downloads/equality_and_justice.doc (Judicial Studies Board's chapter on 'Equality and justice' from the *Equal Treatment Bench Book*)

www.nbpa.co.uk/index.php?option=com_frontpage&Itemid=1 (National Black Police Association)

6 Religion

Introduction

The increasing diversity of British society and the increasing attention given to Islamic fundamentalism in the last decade have caused the police to pay greater attention to matters of religion. Policing diverse communities now no longer solely calls for race to be considered (if it ever did); religious differences are also as relevant, or arguably more relevant. In this chapter, the main religions in the UK will be introduced and their relation to policing will be discussed. There will be a particular focus on two aspects of religious debate. First, attention will be given to the relationship between the police and the Muslim community as that has been a high-profile issue in the last decade. Second, there will be a discussion of the way that the Police Service for Northern Ireland (PSNI) has dealt with sectarianism. Northern Ireland has been dominated by conflict for much of the last 40 years, and this conflict has had a strong religious element, which has had a significant impact on policing practice.

REFLECTIVE TASK

Religious beliefs

Before you start reading this chapter on religion it is worth taking a few minutes to think about your own religious beliefs. Even though most of the exercises in this book can be completed in groups, it might be more appropriate to complete this one individually, as personal matters of religious belief can be quite sensitive.

- *Do you have strong religious or philosophical beliefs?*

- *How do you feel about people who have very different beliefs from yours?*

- *Do you think that people with strong religious beliefs are more or less likely to offend than the general population?*

- *What are your views on how the media report the relationship between religion and offending? In your view, is the reporting generally fair or are the links that are sometimes drawn between, for example, Islam and terrorism, or the Catholic Church and child abuse, unfair to the vast majority of peaceful, law-abiding practitioners of those religions?*

Policy and legislation

In a similar way to the legislation relating to other aspects of diversity, it is also illegal to discriminate against individuals on the basis of their religion or belief. The key legislation relating to employment is the Employment Equality (Religion or Belief) Regulations 2003. The Regulations make it illegal to discriminate by way of:

- *direct discrimination* – to treat people less favourably on the basis of their religion or belief;

- *indirect discrimination* – to apply a criterion or provision, without justification, that would disadvantage someone of a particular religion or belief;

- *harassment* – defined as conduct that creates an environment that is hostile, intimidating, degrading or in other ways offensive;

- *victimisation* – treating someone less favourably because of action they have taken under the Regulations, such as making a complaint or giving evidence.

The Regulations apply to discrimination on the grounds of religion, religious belief or similar philosophical belief. They also apply to beliefs that are both actual and perceived; thus, for example, if someone was treated less favourably because their employer believed that they were a Muslim, they would not actually have to be a Muslim to be covered by the Regulations. Discrimination against associates such as friends and family is also covered.

The Equality Act 2006 also makes it illegal to discriminate against an individual on the basis of religion or belief:

- in employment;
- in the provision of goods or services;
- when providing education or exercising public functions.

The Act also defines religion and belief as needing to be cogent, serious, cohesive and compatible with human dignity. Denominations or sects within religions are also considered to be religions under the Act. Philosophical beliefs such as humanism are covered by the Act, but political affiliation is not.

The Racial and Religious Hatred Act 2006 creates an offence of stirring up hatred against someone because of their religion, giving people the right to protection from hatred on the basis of their religion, as they would have if they had been a victim of racist hate crime. This has, however, been controversial legislation and when it was eventually enacted it included amendments from the House of Lords to reduce its scope, and distinguish it from the legislation on racial hatred. There is now a freedom of expression defence clause and prosecutors must prove that the words, material or behaviour were threatening and that there was an intention to stir up religious hatred (Chakraborti and Garland, 2009).

Criminological and sociological perspectives

Religion in society

Before discussing the link between religion, discrimination and the criminal justice system, it is worthwhile to introduce the main religions in the UK. Information in this section is taken from the BBC website, which is an excellent resource for finding out more about these religions or about others.

Christianity

Christianity is the world's most popular religion; there are over two billion Christians in the world, including six million people in the UK who describe themselves as practising Christians. The core of the Christian faith is the belief that Jesus was the Son of God. Christians follow the teachings of the Bible and the most important dates in their calendar are Easter and Christmas.

Hinduism

Over 900 million people describe themselves as Hindus, and it is the main religion of India and Nepal. Hinduism is more like a family of religions, rather than a single religion, in that there is a variety of key figures in history and a variety of holy books. It is both a cultural and religious identity. The highest-profile Hindu festival is Diwali, the festival of lights, which falls in October or November.

Islam

With over a billion followers, Islam is the second largest religion in the world. Followers of Islam are called Muslims, and there are over 1.5 million in the UK. They believe that there is only one God, Allah, and that God sent prophets to inform humanity of the best way to live, with Muhammad being the last of these prophets. The Qur'an is the Muslim holy book, and the five pillars of Islamic faith are prayer, fasting, giving to the poor, declaring faith and the pilgrimage to Mecca.

Judaism

There are over 13 million Jews in the world, most of whom live the USA and Israel. There are over a quarter of a million Jews in the UK. The religion was founded by Moses, and Jews believe that they have a covenant with God. The Jewish holy book is the Torah. Over six million Jews were murdered by the Nazis in the holocaust.

Sikhism

Most of the 20 million Sikhs in the world come from the Punjab region of India and there are over 300,000 in the UK. The religion emphasises the need to do good works, rather than to simply follow religious rituals, and values the individual's internal spiritual state. Good works include generosity, the promotion of equality, honesty and serving others. The Sikh holy book is the Guru Granth Sahib.

Religious and cultural identity

A religious label can be a statement of what an individual believes but it may also be simply a statement about their background or their culture. This can change, even for one individual, depending on the context. For example, a non-religious white British woman might be most comfortable describing herself as having no religion. However, if she was travelling in North Africa she might be more inclined to identify as 'Christian', as a way of connecting to her family and country of birth. In a similar way, there are many people who might describe themselves as 'British Muslims' or 'British Hindus', who might only have a very loose association with the actual religious faith.

A further complication relates to faiths that are passed on from generation to generation. In both Sikhism and Judaism, someone is initially considered to belong to that faith by virtue of their parentage, rather than being required to declare any personal commitment. As discussed below, this led to an anomaly in the race discrimination legislation, which protected Sikhs and Jews as belonging to racial groups, but did not extend that protection to Muslims or Hindus.

Religious diversity

The list of religions above is clearly not exhaustive or definitive and it is likely that a police officer in his or her career will encounter offenders, victims and members of the public from a variety of religions. Familiarise yourself with the relevant section of the BBC website (www.bbc.co.uk/religion/), so that you are conscious of it as a resource that you can access if necessary.

You can never be fully knowledgeable about and prepared for every situation you might encounter. What principles of good practice might it be useful for a police officer to follow in encountering someone belonging to a particular religion, even if he or she knows nothing of that religion?

Islam and the criminal justice system

Prior to considering the specific matter of the relationship between Islamic communities and the police, it is worth considering the wider context of the relationship between Islam and the criminal justice system. The reason for singling out Islam, rather than considering religion in general, is the particular profile that Islam has and the concerns that have been expressed about Islamophobia in the criminal justice system. This is a relatively recent development and the changing approach to considering race and racism is succinctly summarised by Alexander (2008). She repeats the caricature that race research used to proceed on the premise that the Asians have culture but the West Indians have problems, and this has now mutated into a premise that non-Muslim Asians have culture but Muslims have problems. She argues that Islamophobia should not be considered a new phenomenon, but rather just the latest manifestation of the age-old problem of racism.

In a Runnymede Trust publication, Berkeley argues that the desire for greater engagement between communities could be frustrated by poor community relations:

> *There remains, however, a historical mistrust between minority ethnic communities and the criminal justice system. Through celebrated injustices to daily street harassment, there has been an antipathy developed. All the more tragic since African Caribbean citizens are also more likely to be victims of crime. There are recent reports from community organisations of increasing levels of stop and search on identifiably Muslim youth, which may lead to similar tensions between the police and these communities.*

> *Increasingly the criminal justice system will be relying on community involvement for the lay magistracy, restorative justice, meaningful community sentencing, mentoring, youth justice referral panels, inter alia, against the backdrop of negative relations with large portions of certain communities.*

> (Berkeley, 2004, p5)

In the quotation above, Berkeley makes special reference to what he refers to as 'identifiably Muslim youth'. It is worth noting that particular aspect of diversity. Islam,

Islamophobia and the criminal justice system are areas of increasing concern for society and for criminal justice. As is discussed throughout this book, there is a wealth of material available about some aspects of diversity, such as race and racism, but much less about other aspects, including religion. It is worthwhile to define what we mean when we use the term 'Islam'. To describe someone as Islamic, or as a Muslim, can have three meanings – it can relate to their identity, political ideology or religious faith (Ruthven, 2000).

- *Identity*. A Muslim could be a person born to a Muslim father who takes on the father's identity, without necessarily subscribing to the beliefs and practices of the faith. Such Muslims in non-Muslim societies may have secular identities, for example Muslims in Bosnia. But there is little consistency in how these labels are applied, and the words 'Muslim' and 'Islam' are contested territory everywhere.

- *Political ideology*. The focus of those defending Islam against secularisation is on action, not belief. The means may vary, and may include democratic means in Jordan, or armed conflict in Egypt or Algeria.

- *Religious faith*. A sense of inner commitment links the believer to God in a personal relationship that transcends ritual and law.

As well as the limited research and scholarship on Islam and the police, there is a small body of research concerning probation and Islam. The most significant recent research was carried out by Hudson and Bramhall (2005), who found that the police sometimes acted in a discriminatory way to Muslims, and that probation officers often inadvertently colluded with police discrimination. The researchers found that, in probation reports, adherence to religion and communities is seen as much more of a negative than a positive, and the first association with Muslim Asianness is often the strong web of family bonds and controls. The findings demonstrate that assessments of Muslim Asians reinforce entrenched stereotypes of the strengths of Muslim families and new stereotypes of the aggression of young Asian men. Muslims are seen as 'Other' because of their religion, family and community traditions, in their dress, and in their separateness and strangeness.

> *The effect is a cumulative criminal justice process in which discrimination largely takes the form of disbelief in Muslim Asian accounts and denial of Muslim Asian circumstances.*
>
> (Hudson and Bramhall, 2005, p734)

PRACTICAL TASK

Islam and the criminal justice system

There are three key questions relating to the criminal justice system and Islam. In study groups, discuss your responses to these questions.

- *Do we as individual practitioners know enough about Islam to allow us to work effectively with Muslim offenders? Where has our knowledge come from?*

- *Do we know enough organisationally about Islam and the criminal justice system? Has there been sufficient research and investigation concerning this issue?*

- *Spalek (2002) argues that most anti-discriminatory movements are secular and so ignore issues of religious diversity. Is our anti-discrimination/diversity framework sufficient to deal with issues of Islam and Islamophobia?*

Historical and current police practice

Northern Ireland: from RUC to PSNI

In Northern Ireland, the religious make-up of the police was linked to the contested nature of the state and the role of the police in maintaining it. Since the creation of the state of Northern Ireland in 1922, the police were largely supported by the Protestant Unionist and Loyalist communities, but opposed by the Catholic Nationalist and Republican communities. The police service was known as the Royal Ulster Constabulary (RUC) and had the responsibility both for policing the community and for maintaining the state. The RUC was therefore perceived very differently by the two communities, with the Protestants viewing it as a necessary protector against the aggression of Republicans, and the Catholics viewing it as a representation of a discriminatory state.

Prior to the ceasefires called in 1994, Northern Ireland society was dominated by violent conflict involving Republican and Loyalist terrorists, and the state security services. Throughout the history of Northern Ireland the RUC was overwhelmingly Protestant, despite the fact that one-third of the population of Northern Ireland identified as Catholic. The proportion of Catholics in the police declined from 21 per cent in 1923 to 11 per cent in 1969, and then continued to decline in the following three decades so that, at the end of the 1990s, about 8 per cent of the RUC was Catholic (Mulcahy, 2006, 2008). The RUC was absolutely central to the troubles in Northern Ireland. Its responsibility for protecting the community and its association with the state meant that its members became regular targets for terrorist attacks, with 300 officers murdered between 1968 and 1998 (RUC, 2009). However, the RUC never fully succeeded in gaining the confidence of the Catholic community and faced serious allegations, including those of collusion.

Following the 1998 Belfast Agreement (also known as the Good Friday Agreement), which brought a new, inclusive political dispensation to Northern Ireland, and also brought the troubles to an end, a commission was set up to consider the future of policing. This became known as the Patten Commission, after its chair, Chris Patten. The Patten Report (1999) made a series of recommendations that were all designed to help create a police service that could properly police the community as it moved into a time of peace, despite still being deeply religiously divided in many ways (Mulcahy, 2006).

- Human rights should be fully integrated into the new police service and should be at the core of its philosophy.

- Policing should be a matter for the whole community, and should be based on genuine partnership between the police and the community.

- The police should be accountable to the community and everything should be available for public scrutiny, except where there are specific reasons why this should not happen. New institutions were created to allow this to happen.

- The proposal of the report was for a decentralised and streamlined structure that put community policing at its core.

- The police service should be representative of the community that it serves and, in particular, there should be an increase in the number of Catholics employed. The recommendation was that, for ten years, there should be a 50:50 recruitment of Catholics and Protestants (reflecting the demographic make-up of people in their twenties and thirties in Northern Ireland), with the aim that, at the end of that period, the police service should be 30 per cent Catholic.

- The report recommended that the symbols of the new service should command the support of the whole community and not be closely associated with either the British or Irish state.

The implementation of the Patten Commission's recommendations (1999) led to the formation of the Police Service of Northern Ireland (PSNI). The approach of the PSNI to ensure religious fairness and diversity in its make-up and policing of the community will be discussed in the next section.

REFLECTIVE TASK

Patten recommendations

The Patten recommendations were made at a specific time and in a specific context, but they do reflect contemporary thinking about the nature of policing.

- *How relevant do you think those recommendations are to policing in the rest of the UK?*

- *As the police are seeking to gain the confidence of the Muslim community and other religious groups, are there lessons that could be learned and applied from the Patten recommendations?*

Policing Muslim communities

In discussing the historic and current police practice in policing Muslim communities, Chakraborti (2007) makes the important point that there are two elements to the relationship between the police and the Muslim community. First, the police must protect the Muslim community from hate crime and, second, they must defend the state from an extreme Islamist terrorist threat. Chakraborti (2007) describes the Muslim community in the UK as a diverse community, which is often mistaken for a homogeneous group, and which has grown since the 1950s to a community of around 1.6 million people. The growth in numbers in the Muslim community, along with the increasing tendency of some

British Muslims to consider their religion as the primary aspect of their identity, has seen a parallel growth in Islamophobia. A Runnymede Trust paper in 1997 identified the need to use the term Islamophobia to describe unfounded hostility towards the Muslim community (Runnymede Trust, 1997), which had gone on for many centuries. However, the terrorist attacks of 11 September 2001 in New York and 7 July 2005 in London significantly heightened the problem of anti-Islamic prejudice. Chakraborti (2007) relates figures that indicate that attacks on Muslims increased fourfold in the few weeks after the attacks in New York and sixfold in the weeks after the attacks in London.

REFLECTIVE TASK

Perceived religion

It is worth remembering at this point that the hate crime legislation does not simply protect people who belong to a particular religion; they are also protected if they are attacked because they are perceived to belong to a religion. So Sikhs, Hindus and other Arab and Asian groups who were the victims of Islamophobic violence would still be protected by the legislation, even though they belonged to a different religion, or no religion.

- *Why do you think it is important that hate crime legislation protects people who are perceived to belong to a religion as well as people who actually belong to that religion?*

- *Can you think of any other examples, not necessarily about religion, apart from the one related above, where such protection might be necessary?*

The government and the police do seem to have had some success in responding to hate crime against Muslims, and the new religiously aggravated offences in the Anti-Terrorism, Crime and Security Act 2001 have provided some protection to Muslim communities. However, the attempts to create community cohesion have been less successful. Government community building is often conceptualised as part of a security strategy, so rather than bringing communities together it can send a message of distrust to Muslim communities. From a policing point of view, the anti-terrorist legislation that has been introduced in the last decade has been very controversial and is perceived as being directed at Muslim communities. The provisions against the 'glorifying of terrorism', allowing stop and search and detention without trial, are perceived as having a disproportionately negative effect on Muslim communities. The latter have concerns that they might be targeted because of general assumptions about the risk that they pose, rather than specific intelligence about any specific threat. The concerns that they might be targeted by the police have undermined the good work that is otherwise being done in building community relations and protecting Muslim communities against hate crime (Chakraborti, 2007).

Chakraborti (2007) argues that, in order to achieve community cohesion and enable the Muslims to have confidence in the state, it is important that a good relationship between communities and the police is developed. He quotes research that shows that most Muslims fear police harassment and lack faith in the IPCC. They also feel that the police engage with them solely on police terms, and that the involvement of government ministers is often tokenistic. It is therefore difficult to see much progress in the development of good relationships between the police and the Muslim community, but such relationships are essential to the dual goals of protecting Muslims from hate crime and preventing acts of terrorism by extreme Islamists. Chakraborti (2007) does end with a note of optimism, however – the underlying positive attitude that the Muslim community has towards the police could provide a foundation for future community cohesion work.

REFLECTIVE TASK

Building confidence

Can you think of any steps that the police could take, either locally or nationally, to gain greater confidence from the Muslim community? You should think particularly of good practice in working with other parts of the community that might be applicable to working with Muslims.

Other religious hate crime

Anti-Semitism

Although hate crime against Muslim communities has been a focus of police and media attention, it is important not to neglect the fact that other communities have also been subjected to hate crime. Anti-Semitism has been a prominent feature in history and remains present in modern British society. Chakraborti and Garland (2009) quote research that shows that there has been an increase in anti-Semitic activity in the UK in recent years, and the incidents recorded include some serious assaults. Some of these incidents are associated with far-right extremist groups, but this is not the case for all of them, and many incidents are relatively low-level occurrences, such as name-calling, which can nevertheless have a significant cumulative effect. There is evidence to suggest that events in the Middle East affect the rate of anti-Semitic attacks in the UK, as opposition to Israeli actions may easily translate into hatred of the Jewish community (Chakraborti and Garland, 2009).

Sectarian hate crime, Northern Ireland

The PSNI must deal with the particular issue of sectarian hate crime. Sectarianism is defined as violence, harassment or abuse aimed by members of the Protestant community towards members of the Catholic community, or vice versa. As Chakraborti and Garland (2009) observe, sectarian hate crime is unusual in this respect in that the victim can come from either the majority or the minority community. Although sectarian tension has decreased in Northern Ireland following the Good Friday Agreement and the introduction of the Assembly, sectarian hate crime remains the most common hate crime in Northern Ireland and the incidents have actually increased from 1,000 in the period April to September 2008 to 1,153 in the same period in 2009 (PSNI, 2009b). Worryingly, racist and homophobic hate crime figures are also increasing; racist attacks on Romanian families in Belfast attracted national media attention in 2009. (As always, crime statistics should be treated with caution – an increase in reported incidents may not actually mean that there has been an increase in offending. It is possible that the increase might even be positive, indicating an increased confidence in the police and therefore more reporting of crime.)

At the time of writing, Northern Ireland is experiencing increased dissident terrorist activity, along with some political instability caused by the tension over the devolution of justice powers to the Assembly. History shows that this is likely to lead to the police having to deal with an increase in the incidence of sectarian hate crime.

Best current police practice and plans for the future

The Police Service of Northern Ireland

The recommendations of the Patten Commission (1999) were accepted in principle by the government and implemented in the Police (Northern Ireland) Act 2000. (How closely this Act reflected the views of the Commission was a matter of great debate, but a discussion of this is beyond the scope of this book.) Although the PSNI remains a relatively new organisation, it is clear that it is already a much more attractive career option to Catholics than the RUC was.

Prior to the ceasefires in 1994, Catholics comprised around 11 per cent of applicants to the RUC. This figure did rise following the ceasefires but it took until 2001, and the first recruitment campaign into the new PSNI, for the number of Catholic applicants to reflect in any way the make-up of the population of Northern Ireland. In 2001, approximately 40 per cent of applications were from Catholics and 38 per cent were from women. In 2003, 36 per cent of applicants were Catholic and 37 per cent were women. As these applicants are appointed, trained and then take up fully qualified police officer positions, they slowly change the make-up of the service as a whole, such that, in 2005, 16 per cent of the service comprised Catholics and 19 per cent were women (all figures are from the Northern Ireland Policing Board, quoted in Mulcahy, 2006).

REFLECTIVE TASK

Gender representation

Measures taken to increase the representation of Catholics in the PSNI have also had the effect of increasing the representation of women. Why do you think that might be?

The increase in the representation of women and Catholics in the PSNI has also been accompanied by some change in the culture of the service, and an increase in public confidence in the work of the police. This change has not been without some challenges, with some of the new training on human rights receiving a mixed response from trainee police officers (Mulcahy, 2006). However, the most recent PSNI annual report (PSNI, 2009a) is a good indicator of the priorities of the service, discussing measures that are being taken in working with the community to reduce hate crime and sexual assault. The fact that the report is available in five languages, including Irish, is another indicator of the changes both in Northern Irish society and in its policing, and shows how a police service that was once treated with hostility by part of the community is now working in partnership with all sections of the community.

Religiously aggravated offences

Although the Crime and Disorder Act 1998 deals specifically with racially aggravated offences, the practice, over time, has been to expand this definition to include some religious aggravation. This expansion began with religious groups that largely coincide with ethnic groups, such as the Sikh and Jewish communities, but this led to an anomalous situation in which some religious groups were protected but others were not. Eventually, the Racial and Religious Hatred Act 2006 created an offence of stirring up hatred against someone because of their religion. Legislation to prohibit religiously aggravated offences has always been controversial and contentious, as it is very difficult to frame legislation that does not inhibit the right to free speech. The difficult boundary between prohibiting hatred and promoting free speech was demonstrated in the controversy over the publication of the Danish cartoons in 2006 (see Chakraborti and Garland, 2009, for a discussion of this).

The most prominent example of religiously motivated hate crime relates to Islamophobia, as discussed in the previous section. The alarmist language used by both the media and politicians has led to increased hostility towards Muslims and an increasing division between them and members of other ethnic minority groups (Chakraborti and Garland, 2009).

It is also important to note that religion can play a role in creating and reinforcing the ideological conditions that lead to hate crime. Hall (2005) identifies religion as one of three ideologies that lead to extreme hate crime, and some extreme hate groups adopt a corrupted version of a Christian identity, which provides a theological rationale for their hate-based offending behaviour.

Police employees and religion

As with all other aspects of diversity, the police need to respond to religious differences both in their relationships with the community and in how they work as an organisation. The growing diversity of society and the recruiting policies of the police have led to an increasingly diverse profile of the police organisation. Associations have been formed to represent the interests of different religious groups within the police.

The National Association of Muslim Police
There has been an increasing emphasis on recruiting a police service that has a similar profile to the community it serves. This, combined with the increase in the Muslim population, has led to higher numbers of Muslim police officers, and the formation of a National Association of Muslim Police (NAMP). The NAMP was set up to represent the

interests of all Muslim staff within the police, and its website states that its key objectives are to:

- provide a support network for Muslim staff in the police;

- improve community cohesion and increase trust and confidence in the police;

- address issues of recruitment and retention of Muslim staff in the police;

- raise awareness of Islamic issues and Islamophobia.

The NAMP organises conferences and other events, provides mentoring and support, and carries out research. One important piece of research carried out by the NAMP, in partnership with the think tank Demos, was to map the distribution of Muslim police officers across the country (Demos/NAMP, 2008). The police are not required by law to monitor the religious make-up of constabularies, although they are required to record figures for race, disability and gender. This report found that Muslims are under-represented in the police, as they make up less than 1 per cent of the police force, compared to 3 per cent of the wider population. The report suggests that further research is required to establish the reasons for this under-representation, but speculates that the reasons could include institutional discrimination or unwillingness on the part of Muslims to consider careers in the police. The report makes four recommendations to help achieve the goal of higher representation of Muslims in the police (Demos/NAMP, 2008).

- There needs to be an understanding of why Muslims are currently under-represented. Data needs to be collected systematically on a national level.

- Positive action is taking place in a number of forces, but this needs to be better publicised, promoted and replicated. There needs to be a communication plan in place to promote positive action.

- There should be a priority in recruiting and training Muslim officers to work in counter-terrorism. Having police officers who have a cultural, linguistic and religious under-standing of individuals targeted for recruitment by Al-Qaeda would be extremely valuable. Utilising Muslim officers in this way would benefit both the Muslim community and the police.

- The Home Office should devise an action plan to progress the issues from the report.

Although the NAMP has received official approval, with both Gordon Brown and Ronnie Flanagan addressing its most recent conference, its work is not universally welcomed. For example, Rowe (2008) raises the concern that associations such as the NAMP and the Black Police Association might simply highlight how overwhelmingly white the police organisation is and marginalise the issues facing members of these groups. This echoes the same writer's earlier concern that Police Community Race Relations training had an unhelpful tendency to identify one leader of a particular group, such as the Sikh community, and seek a definitive understanding of the community's policing needs from that one person (Rowe, 2004).

REFLECTIVE TASK

Muslims in the police

- Do you know any Muslim police officers, or Muslims who would like to join the police? Perhaps you belong to one of these categories yourself. Why do you think there are not more Muslims in the police?

- Do you think it is likely to be discrimination, lack of interest from the Muslim community or a combination of both?

- Apart from the points stated above, can you think of any other potential benefits in having more Muslims in the police?

- Look back at your answers to the previous exercises regarding the PSNI. Are there any steps that were taken to address the under-representation of the Catholic community in Northern Ireland that could be applied to the Muslim community in Great Britain?

The experience of Muslims in the police received national attention in 2008 in the case of Assistant Commissioner of the Metropolitan Police, Tarique Ghaffur. Ghaffur made a claim of racial discrimination against the Metropolitan Police, and this included claims that the then Commissioner, Sir Ian Blair, acted in a racist way. Ghaffur ultimately agreed an out-of-court settlement and withdrew his claims.

The NAMP is the highest-profile religious group in the police, but it is not the only one. Information about the NAMP and the other religious associations has been obtained from their websites (links appear at the end of the chapter) and these groups include the following.

The Christian Police Association

The Christian Police Association (CPA) has been in existence since 1883 and is part of a worldwide network of such organisations. According to its website, the aim of the CPA is to encourage and support Christians in the police, communicate their faith to others and build links between the police, the churches and other Christian community groups. Regional networks allow members to identify and meet with Christian colleagues. In contrast to some of the other religious associations in the police, the CPA has an outward focus in seeking to persuade others to adopt the Christian faith. It is located within the evangelical tradition of Christianity (it is a member of the Evangelical Alliance) and asks its members to be 'born again' Christians. In common with other churches and organisations in the evangelical tradition, it describes itself as non-denominational, but it does not attract Catholics.

The CPA entered into a public dispute with the Gay Police Association (GPA) in 2006 that received national media attention. The CPA objected to a GPA advert that stated that religion was a primary motivation behind much homophobic hate crime. The advert included a picture of a Bible, next to a pool of blood. The GPA in turn objected to the CPA's insistence that a gay, Christian police officer become celibate before joining the organisation.

The Catholic Police Guild

The Guild was formed in 1914 in the Metropolitan Police, and is still mainly London-based, with a branch in the north-west, but no established regional network. It aims to provide support and fellowship, and also encourages members to act with integrity and strength of character. The Guild holds annual events, including a Mass and a Retreat, to help all members reflect on their faith. It also provides more informal, social events.

The British Sikh Police Association and the Metropolitan Sikh Police Association

There are two organisations that represent Sikhs in the police and they take slightly different approaches. The British Sikh Police Association (BSPA) was launched in April 2009. Its aims include providing support for Sikhs in the police, promoting integration and understanding of the Sikh faith, and aiding recruitment, retention and progression. The Metropolitan Sikh Police Association (MSPA) has just two aims: advancing the Sikh religion and promoting the efficiency of the Metropolitan Police.

One of the issues that has led to debate regarding Sikhs in the police is the wearing of turbans. Sikhs who wear turbans are currently not able to join firearms units, as they are prohibited by their religion from removing their turbans to wear helmets. Shortly after its formation, the BSPA called on the Home Office to make bullet-proof turbans available. The issue was further highlighted later in 2009, when a Sikh police officer won compensation from Greater Manchester Police after he was obliged to remove his turban during a training course.

The Jewish Police Association

The Jewish Police Association (JPA) offers support and advice to Jewish employees within the police, as well as promoting the image and reputation of the police within the Jewish community. It regularly organises campaigns within the Jewish community to promote employment opportunities within the police. It is based in a variety of police forces, but has a particularly close relationship with the Metropolitan Police. In March 2009 the JPA held a joint event with the National Police Improvement Agency (NPIA) to raise awareness of issues of interest to Jewish officers.

The Metropolitan Hindu Police Association

The Metropolitan Hindu Police Association (MPHA) was formed in 2002 with the aims of providing support to Hindus working within the police, improving recruitment and retention, and influencing policy. It also hopes to influence members of the Hindu community to consider a career in the police.

PRACTICAL TASK

Faith organisations

The organisations described above all perform important roles in supporting police staff of particular religious persuasions, and of promoting understanding of faith groups within the police and vice versa. Some of these groups also see their role as promoting integrity and honesty in police practice. However, they also have some potentially negative consequences in entrenching difference between groups and in encouraging the idea that faith groups are homogeneous and that their interests can be represented by one organisation or even one spokesperson. The disagreement between the GPA and the CPA highlights the fact that promoting diversity is sometimes complicated, in that the interests of different groups can sometimes be in conflict with each other.

* *What is your view of the many police organisations that support individual religious groups? You may wish to look at some of the websites listed at the end of the chapter before making up your mind.*

* *Do you think they are necessary and valuable sources of support and information, or potentially divisive, narrowly focused interest groups?*

Hate crime

The increase in religiously motivated hate crime has led to the introduction of new legislation, the Racial and Religious Hatred Act 2006, but this has proved controversial both to enact and to implement. Before the enactment of this legislation in 2006, there had been seven attempts in the previous 12 years to introduce the same legal protection for those who had been subjected to religiously motivated hate crime as was available to those who had been the victims of racist hate crime (Chakraborti and Garland, 2009). The situation was particularly anomalous, as some religious groups could be included in the definition of a racial group (such as Sikhs and Jews) while others were excluded from that definition (such as Christians and Muslims). Other justifications for the introduction of such legislation were that it would send a signal about society's rejection of such hatred; it could curtail the activities of far-right extremists; and it could also restrain some of the extremist rhetoric from within parts of the Muslim community (Chakraborti and Garland, 2009).

It proved to be difficult to frame religious hatred legislation successfully and the legislation that was eventually enacted was worded in a weaker way than had originally been proposed. Concerns about the curtailing of freedom of expression led to the legislation only criminalising words or behaviour that were deliberately threatening, and that were intended to engender religious hatred. Behaviour that was merely abusive or insulting was excluded from the legislation, and this meant that the law differed from that concerning the incitement of racial hatred. The offence thus created was therefore one that was very hard to prove, in that it required proof of the subjective intent of the accused to incite hatred. In practice, many of the people who were intended to be caught by this legislation, such as far-right extremists, are able to frame their words in such a way that what they say is not covered by the legislation (Chakraborti and Garland, 2009).

Inciting religious hatred

In November 2009, a Christian couple, Benjamin and Sharon Vogelenzang, were pros-ecuted for inciting religious hatred against a Muslim woman, Erica Tazi, who was a guest at their bed and breakfast establishment. The couple contested the charges. Ms Tazi alleged that they had made insulting statements about Islam and the prophet Muhammad, and that insulting statements were made to her simply because she was a Muslim. Mr and Mrs Vogelenzang denied this version of events, alleged that Ms Tazi had herself made offensive statements about their religion, and claimed the right to freedom of speech.

All charges were dismissed by the court soon after the case started, but the Vogelenzangs told the court that their business takings were down by 80 per cent due to the bad publicity they had received, and due to the fact that the hospital that had recommended them to Ms Tazi no longer recommended them to out-patients. Following media criticism, the CPS was forced to justify its decision to bring the prosecution.

It is worth noting that the Vogelenzangs were not charged under the Racial and Religious Hatred Act 2006, but under section 5 of the Public Order Act 1986 and sections 31 (1)(c) and 31 (5) of the Crime and Disorder Act 1998.

Legislation on religious hatred has been devised as a necessary compromise between the need to protect religious communities from hatred and abuse, and the requirement to protect freedom of speech in a free society. These issues are emotive and contentious, and the risks and difficulties of bringing a successful prosecution are demonstrated by the Vogelenzang case.

- *Do you think it is fair to bring the police into these debates?*

- *Are the police and the CPS equipped to make the sort of judgements that were required in considering the decision to prosecute the Vogelenzangs?*

C H A P T E R   S U M M A R Y

The issue of religion and policing is relevant both to the relationship between the police and the community and to the treatment of police employees within the organisation. This is similar to other strands of diversity, but there are some factors that apply in a different way to religion. First, the history of sectarian conflict in Northern Ireland and the integral way in which policing has been central to that conflict means that religious diversity in Northern Ireland is especially highly charged and crucial. Second, the attention given to the place of Muslims in British society and the need both to protect society from extremist Islamic terrorism and to protect Muslims from hate crime has placed a particular focus on Muslims and policing. Third, considering religious differences highlights one of the most difficult issues in diversity practice – how to respond when the interests of different groups appear to be in conflict. The association drawn by the Gay Police Association between the Christian faith and homophobia angered Christian police officers, and it is difficult to see how that issue could be resolved to everyone's satisfaction.

However, the best diversity practice of sensitivity, gaining as much information about individuals and groups as possible, and avoiding making assumptions should usually be just as effective an approach to religious diversity as to the other strands.

REFERENCES

Alexander, C (2008) Introduction to the Asian Gang, in Spalek, B (ed.) *Ethnicity and Crime: A Reader*. Maidenhead: McGraw-Hill.

Berkeley, R (2004) *Runnymede Perspectives: Civil Renewal for All*. London: Runnymede Trust.

Chakraborti, N (2007) Policing Muslim communities, in Rowe, M (ed.) *Policing Beyond Macpherson*. Cullompton: Willan.

Chakraborti, N and Garland, J (2009) *Hate Crime: Impact, Causes and Responses*. London: Sage.

Demos/NAMP (2008) *Diversity in Modern Policing*. Available online at www.demos.co.uk/publications (accessed 15 August 2009).

Hall, N (2005) *Hate Crime*. Cullompton: Willan.

Hudson, B and Bramhall, G (2005) Assessing the other: constructions of 'Asianness' in risk Assessments by probation officers. *British Journal of Criminology*, 45: 721–40.

Mulcahy, A (2006) *Policing Northern Ireland: Conflict, Legitimacy and Reform*. Cullompton: Willan.

Mulcahy, A (2008) Police Service of Northern Ireland, in Newburn, T and Neyroud, P (eds) *Dictionary of Policing*. Cullompton: Willan.

Patten, C (1999) *A New Beginning: Policing in Northern Ireland. The Report of the Independent Commission on Policing in Northern Ireland.* Belfast: Stationery Office.

Police Service of Northern Ireland (PSNI) (2009a) *Chief Constable's Annual Report*. Available online at www.psni.police.uk/index.htm (accessed 15 August 2009).

Police Service of Northern Ireland (PSNI) (2009b) Quarterly hate incidents and crime statistics, April to September 2009. Available online at www.psni.police.uk/index.htm (accessed 15 August 2009).

Rowe, M (2004) *Policing, Race and Racism*. Cullompton: Willan.

Rowe, M (2008) *Introduction to Policing*. London: Sage.

Royal Ulster Constabulary (RUC) (2009) *The Royal Ulster Constabulary George Cross: Memorial*. Available online at www.royalulsterconstabulary.org/memorial.htm (accessed 15 March 2010).

Runnymede Trust (1997) *Islamophobia: A Challenge for Us All*. London: Runnymede Trust.

Ruthven, M (2000) *Islam: A Very Short Introduction*. Oxford: Oxford University Press.

Spalek, B (2002) *Islam, Crime and Criminal Justice*. Cullompton: Willan.

The Demos/NAMP report, *Diversity in Modern Policing* (2008), is a good summary of the issues currently facing Muslims in the police. Much of the material referred to in the chapter on race is also relevant to religion, particularly the assessments of the impact of the Stephen Lawrence Inquiry, ten years on. Aoghan Mulcahy's book, *Policing Northern Ireland* (2006), provides a good coverage of the important issues in Northern Ireland policing, and Basia Spalek's book, *Islam, Crime and Criminal Justice* (2002), is a useful introduction to the issues relating to the Muslim community.

www.bbc.co.uk/religion/ (if you are unfamiliar with the history, origins or basic tenets of the faiths discussed in this chapter, this website contains an excellent introduction to all major world religions)

www.runnymedetrust.org/ (the Runnymede Trust is an organisation with a mandate to promote a successful multi-ethnic Britain. It has published a lot of material on religion and criminal justice)

Some of the specific religious groups mentioned in this chapter have websites that serve as resources for their members and other interested parties:

http://catholicpoliceguild.org.uk/ (Catholic Police Guild)

www.cpauk.net/ (Christian Police Association)

www.jewishpoliceassociation.org.uk/ (Jewish Police Association)

www.namp-uk.com/home.html (National Association of Muslim Police)

www.redhotcurry.com/ (the Hindu Police Association does not have its own website and information about this organisation was obtained from RedhotCurry.com, which provides news and information for the South Asian community living in the UK)

www.sikhnet.com/home (the British Sikh Police Association does not have its own website, so information about the BSPA was obtained from Sikhnet, which is dedicated to sharing the Sikh experience in the UK)

www.sikhpolice.org/ (Metropolitan Sikh Police Association)

7 Sexual orientation

CHAPTER OBJECTIVES

By the end of this chapter you should be able to:

- describe the key legislation relating to sexual orientation;
- outline the development of criminological and sociological responses to sexual orientation;
- explain the changing relationship between the police and the lesbian, gay and bisexual (LGB) community.

LINKS TO STANDARDS

This chapter provides the following links to Skills for Justice, National Occupational Standards (NOS) for Policing and Law Enforcement 2008.

AB1	Communicate effectively with people.
BE2	Provide initial support to victims, survivors and witnesses and assess their need for further support.
CA1	Use law enforcement actions in a fair and justified way.
HB11	Promote equality of opportunity and diversity in your area of responsibility.

Introduction

The consideration of sexual orientation as one of the strands of diversity is a relatively recent development, and it still commands less attention than some of the other diversity strands. It is an interesting strand to consider because the journey to equal treatment is quite different from that of the other strands discussed in this book. Although discrimination on the basis of, for example, race or gender has been both longstanding and wide-ranging, it has never actually been illegal to simply be black or to be a woman. Gay communities are different from other minority communities in that, in the past, their private sexual lives were subjected to police scrutiny (Chakraborti and Garland, 2009).

In this chapter you will study the progress that has been made from a time when adults were prosecuted for engaging in consensual sexual relationships with other adults of the same gender, to the current situation where gay relationships are not just legal but are actively protected by legislation. You will see how the role of the police has changed from prosecuting and, in some cases, harassing the gay community to participating in Gay Pride marches and taking a lead in employment best practice.

Policy and legislation

It is interesting to note that, although legislation to outlaw sexual and racial discrimination dates from the 1970s, legislation outlawing discrimination on the basis of sexual orientation is much more recent and was introduced by the Labour government that came to power in 1997. Indeed, it was only in 1967 that the Sexual Offences Act decriminalised consensual sexual activity between two males aged over 21.

European Community Directive 2000/78/ EC of 27 November 2000 established a general framework for equal treatment in employment, so far as it relates to discrimination on the grounds of sexual orientation, and includes direct discrimination, indirect discrimination, victimisation and harassment. On 1 December 2003 sexual orientation legislation came into force in the form of the Employment Equality (Sexual Orientation) Regulations 2003.

For the purposes of these Regulations, a person (A) discriminates against another person (B):

- directly – when A treats B less favourably than he or she treats or would treat other persons;

- indirectly – when A applies to B a provision, criterion or practice which he or she applies or would apply equally to persons not of the same sexual orientation as B, but:

  - which puts or would put persons of the same sexual orientation as B at a particular disadvantage when compared with other persons;

  - which puts B at that disadvantage; and

  - which A cannot show to be a proportionate means of achieving a legitimate aim.

In addition, the legislation outlaws harassment, so it is illegal to create a working environment that would be uncomfortable for LGB employees.

Other legislation that has particular reference to the LGB community is the Civil Partnership Act 2005, which affords the same protection to couples in a civil partnership as that given to a married couple. The Sexual Orientation Regulations that were introduced as a consequence of the Equality Act 2007 provide protection to gay people in the provision of goods, facilities and services.

Protection against homophobic hate crime is provided by the Criminal Justice Act 2003. Section 146 of this Act allowed courts to impose heavier sentences where either homophobic hostility or motivation is present. Section 74 of the Criminal Justice and Immigration Act 2008 also creates an offence of inciting hatred based on a person's sexual orientation. The threshold for this offence is set quite high to include threatening behaviour, but it excludes comedy or religious instruction that criticises homosexual conduct (Chakraborti and Garland, 2009).

Criminological and sociological theory

Criminological accounts of sexual orientation have tended to centre on analysis of why male homosexual acts have been criminalised, and whether this is appropriate. The relative scarcity of writing on this subject, however, has led some writers (see Groombridge, 1999, 2006) to criticise criminology for its silence on the matter of discriminatory legislation and its acceptance of the normality of heterosexual relationships.

REFLECTIVE TASK

Language

As you have seen throughout this book, the question of language and definitions is often a difficult one, for example it is difficult to specify who is included or excluded by such terms as 'black', 'Muslim' or 'young person'. This is especially sensitive with regard to sexual orientation, where there is debate regarding the choice of a term that is sufficiently inclusive to take account of all the relevant groups but exclusive enough to be a meaningful definition. This chapter uses the term LGB as shorthand for lesbian, gay and bisexual, following the lead of Stonewall (see below for a discussion of Stonewall), but even that organisation sometimes uses the term LGBT (lesbian, gay, bisexual and trans-gender) on its website.

You are asked to think carefully about language throughout this book, and during your work on equality and diversity. Language used to discuss sexuality and sexual orientation is interesting in that much of the now commonly accepted language, and language used by gay men and lesbians to describe themselves, started out as terms of abuse. The two most prominent examples of this are the terms 'gay' and 'queer'. This can be confusing, particularly as the terms are still used by some as terms of abuse.

- *What are the advantages and disadvantages of using the terms 'lesbian and gay', 'LGB' and 'LGBT'?*

- *Is it accurate to describe the LGB community as a community?*

- *Do you feel comfortable talking about, say, the Gay Police Association? What about Groombridge's use of the term 'queer theory'? If not, why not?*

- *Is the term 'straight', as used to describe people who are heterosexual, equally problematic?*

Groombridge (1999) presents a 'queer' history of criminology, expressing disappointment that criminology has often left homosexuality to law and medicine. He says that the 'common sense' notion of equating homosexuality with crime and treason has pervaded criminology (see Chapter 1 for a discussion of 'common sense'). He notes a number of points at which sexual orientation might have been considered.

- At its earliest point, criminology started by seeking biological explanations for criminal behaviour. Lombroso carried out experiments on offenders and hypothesised that criminal behaviour was linked to such factors as the size of jaws or ears, or the look in people's eyes. These theories are now considered to have no credibility, but Lombroso is widely regarded as the father of criminology. Groombridge speculates on Lombroso's motivations for spending his career carrying out physical examinations of young men. He also notes the link between the origins of criminology, in seeking physical explanations for criminal behaviour, and the early sexologists who sought explanations for sexual orientation using the same methods.

- Groombridge identifies that the tendency of criminology and sociology to focus on what he provocatively terms 'nuts, sluts and perverts', rather than, say, the crimes of the powerful, did lead to an interest in male homosexual behaviour and an attempt to explain it, which was never entirely separate from the dominant assumptions and prejudices of the time.

- Criminologists did, however, contribute positively to arguments that homosexual behaviour should be decriminalised so that police resources could be better used elsewhere. Groombridge relates an incident from 1970 in which a criminological researcher, researching the behaviour of gay men in a public toilet, was arrested while carrying out the research. The researcher noted that, on the day that he was arrested by two experienced senior police officers, three major bank robberies were carried out in the same city.

- Groombridge also expresses disappointment that some strands of criminology, such as feminist criminology and the study of men who offend, have paid so little attention to sexual orientation. He analyses indexes of key criminological textbooks in those traditions and finds that lesbian contributions are glossed over and that the main issues relating to gay men treat them as victims, or potential drug takers, or else concentrate on debates relating to the age of consent. He is unable to find anything that he would consider to be a true 'queer perspective'.

- With particular reference to the police, Groombridge identifies how detailed statistics regarding sexual orientation have never been kept by the police, but questions whether such recording might be beneficial or detrimental. He also suggests that an interesting piece of research might have been to ascertain the experiences of police officers who have been asked to work undercover in order to police public toilets. How might it have felt to be both an object of desire and an agent of social control?

Police practice

Groombridge's analysis of the history of criminology does have some direct relevance to policing.

- *If all victims of crime and all arrested alleged offenders were asked to reveal their sexual orientation, how could that contribute to the achievement of equality?*

- *Conversely, what might be the limitations and dangers of gathering information in this way?*

Patrolling public toilets is not a task that the police have routinely carried out for many years; the Sexual Offences Act 2003 decriminalised buggery and gross indecency and effectively brought this practice to an end. Now, if there are concerns in particular localities, the issue is more likely to be dealt with through public health. It is, however, an important issue to think about when considering the history of the relationship between the gay community and the police.

- *What do you think of the argument that patrolling public toilets and prosecuting consensual sexual activities between adult men is a waste of police resources?*

- *Can you think of any good reasons why the police should deploy resources in this way?*

- *If you do not think it is a proper activity for the police to be spending time on, how would you react if, as a police officer, you were asked to participate in such an investigation? You should bear in mind that, as a serving officer, you would not be permitted to simply pick and choose which orders to carry out.*

Some writers have linked this discussion to their consideration of gender and the dominance of male perspectives in criminology and criminal justice. For example, Walklate (2004) discusses the concepts of normative heterosexuality and hegemonic masculinity, which she defines as follows.

- *Hegemonic masculinity*: the ideas, values and practices associated with being male that are given a powerful position in society.

- *Normative heterosexuality*: the form of masculinity that is valued and given a powerful position in everyday life, so requiring every man to live up to its expectations.

The author says that this powerful status is achieved and maintained in three ways:

- the dominant idea of the man as the breadwinner;

- the definition of homosexuality and not lesbianism as a crime;

- the objectification by the media of heterosexual women.

Walklate (2004) says that these assumptions and expectations have the effect of downgrading and devaluing both femininity and other expressions of masculinity, such as homosexuality.

There have been direct legislative attempts to restrict the expression of homosexuality in society, with the most notorious of these being 'section 28'.

Section 28 of the Local Government Act in England and Wales 1988, usually referred to simply as 'section 28', was introduced by the Conservative government in response to a campaign in the tabloid press relating to some teaching materials allegedly provided in primary schools. The legislation prohibited local authorities from 'promoting' homosexuality. The significant aspect of the legislation was not that it was strictly enforced, but rather that it led to a climate in which teachers were afraid to discuss sexual orientation with children, and even afraid to challenge homophobic bullying. The organisation Stonewall was formed specifically to campaign against section 28, and in 2003 the legislation was repealed by the Labour government.

The dominant position of heterosexuality and the assumptions that are made have also led to the neglect of some sorts of offending. Walklate (2004) describes how offences of rape between men and rape between women are often more invisible even than marital rape or so-called date rape. She quotes research to show that the characteristics of the offenders and the excuses and rationalisations that they provide for their offending are often very similar to those provided by offenders who rape women. Importantly, the research challenges the assumption that men who rape other men are homosexual; in fact, most identify as heterosexual. Offenders commit these offences because they feel they can get away with them, and the legal complexities, as well as the shame and perceived social stigma felt by victims of male rape, means that this is even more strongly the case with regard to rape offences committed by men on male victims.

Same-sex domestic violence is another example of an offence that is sometimes ignored, and this lack of attention makes it even more difficult for victims of such offences to seek support and a police response. Same-sex domestic violence has been recognised by the criminal law since the Domestic Violence, Crime and Victims Act 2003. This offending has to be understood within the context of discrimination and oppression in society. It is difficult to discuss violence in a relationship with anyone else, including a health or criminal justice professional, and this difficulty is exacerbated if the individual also feels unable to disclose his or her sexual orientation (Stonewall, 2009).

Historical police practice

As Rowe (2008) identifies, the relationship between LGB communities and policing has been neglected until very recently. The number of LGB officers has not been systematically monitored and, indeed, this would have been extremely difficult, as many officers might not choose to be open about their sexual orientation. It is only very recently that the age of consent has been equalised between heterosexual and homosexual relationships, so prior to that police officers who identified as lesbian or gay faced an additional difficulty in deciding whether to be open about their sexual orientation at work. Police officers, particularly those who had joined the force at a young age, might be reluctant to discuss their own sexual orientation or even to challenge instances of homophobia in case it revealed past or present criminal behaviour.

REFLECTIVE TASK

Openness and privacy

- *Should police officers who are gay, lesbian or bisexual be open about their sexual orientation at work?*

- *What are the arguments for them being open?*

- *What are the reasons why they might choose not to discuss their sexual orientation?*

- *People have different attitudes to discussing their private life at work. What is your own view on this? Do you like talking about your private life at work (or among fellow students)?*

- *Can you think of other circumstances or situations where an individual might choose not to discuss their private life among work colleagues?*

Rowe (2008) describes how the same arguments are used to justify discrimination against gay police officers that are used to justify discrimination against members of other groups. It is suggested that they are members of a 'deviant' subgroup and that their lifestyle might make it difficult for them to discharge their duties properly. These arguments had particular power before the changes in legislation during the last decade.

Burke (1994) carried out research with LGB police officers (although he used the term non-heterosexual) in the 1990s, before the legislative changes and some of the social changes that took place in the early twenty-first century. He argued that, at that time, homosexuality was considered 'distinctively deviant' in the police and he suggested five reasons why that might be the case.

- *Machismo*. Police culture emphasised sexism, alcohol and sport as ways for police officers to be seen to be strong and manly. Homosexuality struck against that culture and left gay men concerned that they might not be perceived as suitable officers if they were open about their sexual orientation.

- *Lesbianism*. At that time, lesbians seemed to have an easier experience in the police than gay men. They did not face the same possible criminal sanctions (female homosexuality was never specifically criminalised) and the general, perceived image of lesbians was less threatening to police culture. However, lesbian officers feared being open about their sexual orientation as it might hinder their promotion prospects.

- *Impact of the criminal law*. The combination of the impact of the Sexual Offences Act 1967 (which set out the conditions by which consensual sex between adult men would be legal), section 28 of the Local Government Act 1988 (described earlier) and the Criminal Justice Act 1991 (which imposed harsher sentences for serious sexual offences, including some consensual offences) meant that homosexuality was linked to criminality. It was difficult for LGB police officers to reconcile their identity with the way that they knew the gay community was perceived by the police. It was often the case that the only contact that there was between the gay community and the police was when the police were investigating public order, drugs or other offences. The uncertain legal status of gay relationships could have led to an association in the minds of police officers, whether themselves gay or not, between being gay and engaging in criminal activity.

- *Ambivalence.* LGB police officers will have grown up in a society that was homophobic and discriminatory, so will feel ambivalent and conflicted about their own identity. It is unavoidable that they will have internalised some of these messages, and the culture of the police will contribute to this.

- *Double lives.* Police officers who were not open about their sexual orientation had to lead double lives, in that they would have to pretend to be heterosexual at work. There may even have been an extra layer to this deception, as many officers also felt a need to disguise their jobs in the evenings. This lifestyle, with its regular secrets and evasions, would take a psychological and emotional toll on LGB police officers. Burke's (1994) research found that LGB police officers were at risk with regard to their mental health, their relationships and their ability to function comfortably within the police.

Hate crime

Although members of the gay community have suffered harassment and victimisation for some time, it is only recently that this has been taken seriously by the criminal justice system, and that incidents have been properly recorded. In almost the same way that police practice and race relations are dominated by the murder of Stephen Lawrence and the subsequent Inquiry, any discussion of the relationship between the police and the LGB community must take account of the bombing of the Admiral Duncan. The Gay Police Association (GPA) has described this as a 'tipping point' (quoted in Blackbourn, 2006, p30). In April 1999 a nail bomb exploded in the Admiral Duncan pub in Soho, London, killing three adults, including a pregnant woman. This pub was well known as a popular venue for the LGB community. Subsequently, a Nazi sympathiser called David Copeland was convicted of this attack and two other bombings, which were an attempt to stoke up racial and homophobic tensions.

The police response to the Admiral Duncan bombing went some way towards persuading the LGB community that the police were there to protect and support them. The Metropolitan Police consulted with the GPA from an early stage of this investigation and used their 'critical incidents coordinators' to work alongside the senior police officers at the crime scene. The GPA noted with approval:

This was the first time that a large group of lesbian and gay police officers had been operationally deployed to support a police force anywhere in the world and represented a defining moment of police relations with the gay community within the UK.

(Martis, 2005, quoted in Blackbourn, 2006, p30)

The enactment of the Criminal Justice Act 2003, with its section 146 powers to increase sentences for offences motivated by homophobia, was another significant step in providing protection from homophobic assaults. The power of this legislation was demonstrated almost immediately in the case of Jody Dobrowski. Jody Dobrowski was a known gay man who was killed on Clapham Common by two strangers shouting homophobic insults. It was treated as a homophobic assault from the start by both the police and the CPS, and the perpetrators were convicted and sentenced to 28 years each; the sentences were enhanced because of the homophobic aggravation. The men were sentenced on the day the legislation was enacted (Chakraborti and Garland, 2009). Although murder is at the most serious end of homophobic crimes, other offences can include verbal harassment, damage to property and assault.

Best current practice and plans for the future

There is a clear relationship between the changes in police culture relating to LGB officers, and the response of the police to homophobic incidents. As the police have become more open to accepting LGB officers, so they have presented an image of being more inclined to treat homophobic hate crime in a more serious way.

One of the clearest manifestations of the change in the relationship between the gay community and the police is seen in the GPA, which was formed in 1990 in the Metropolitan Police and now has members in all 52 UK police forces. It is mandated by the Home Office to assist in the development of gay policing issues. The purpose of the GPA is to:

- work towards equal opportunities for gay employees of the police;

- give advice and support to employees of the police who are gay;

- promote good relationships between the gay community and the police service.

The GPA contributes to educating the government and the police as well as participating in training and policy development. The Association is called on to provide support and specialist advice when there are incidents of homophobic hate crime (Newburn, 2008).

The most prominent and visible sign of the change in attitudes towards gay police officers has been the response of senior police managers to requests from LGB officers to participate in Gay Pride festivals. The general rule for police officers is that they should not participate in marches or other activities that might be perceived as political. It was initially determined that Gay Pride marches were included in the definition of political events, so it would not be appropriate for police officers to participate. However, after representations from the GPA and others, the police accepted the argument that these events were a celebration of culture, not a political activity. In 2003 over 80 police officers attended the annual Gay Pride march in London, many in full uniform (Rowe, 2008). This practice has been repeated at all annual marches since that date, with the police parading in uniform and also providing stands to advertise their work and attract potential recruits.

One of the ways in which the police have sought to address the difficulties of their past relationships with the gay community is through a relationship with the campaigning organisation, Stonewall. Stonewall has its origins in the campaign against section 28 (see page 130) in 1989. It soon widened its focus to campaign against any form of discrimination against the LGB community, and to promote equal treatment. Stonewall is best known as a campaigning organisation and counts among its successes: the equalisation of the age of consent; repealing the ban on gay men and lesbians in the armed forces; changing the legislation to allow gay men and lesbians to adopt; and the repeal of section 28. The organisation also provides educational resources, produces research reports and provides support for employers who are seeking to achieve equality in the workplace. Stonewall states that its key priorities for 2008/9 are:

- challenging homophobia in schools and addressing underachievement of gay and lesbian pupils;

- continuing to promote equality at work and to highlight good practice;

- promoting fair treatment of LGB people in all areas of the public domain;

- securing further equal legal treatment;

- promoting fair and positive coverage of LGB issues in the media.

The police have made great progress as employers in their approach to LGB officers, to the extent that 13 of the top 100 gay-friendly employers identified by Stonewall in 2007 were police forces (Rowe, 2008). These forces demonstrated that they had good support networks and appropriate human resource processes, and that their senior leaders championed and promoted sexual orientation diversity throughout the organisation (Rowe, 2008). In 2009 three police forces were in Stonewall's top ten (Hampshire Constabulary in second place, Kent Police in fourth and Merseyside Police in eighth), with 22 forces in the top 100, along with the Home Office, the Ministry of Justice and the Ministry of Defence Police and Guarding Agency.

It is worthwhile to consider the case of Hampshire Constabulary in some more detail as it seems to exemplify good police practice. Hampshire Constabulary's website displays its commitment to policing with the LGB community, under the following strapline:

Being lesbian, gay, bisexual or transgender is not a crime – hate crime is.

The Constabulary encourages both the reporting of offences and the logging of them as hate crime. As well as explaining why this is important, the force provides a form that can be completed by those who might be unwilling to visit a police station. It also provides a list of partner organisations that would be prepared to receive a report.

Hampshire Constabulary has introduced Lesbian and Gay Liaison Officers (LAGLOs) who have been specially trained in LGB issues. They aim to enhance the relationship between the police and the gay community, as well as providing specialist advice to their colleagues. They also aim to build trust and confidence through such initiatives as visiting gay-friendly venues. The Constabulary, however, makes it clear that this work is not to be seen as a task for a small group of specialists, but that all officers in the Constabulary should be comfortable with homophobic issues.

The Constabulary has also established the Hampshire Lesbian, Gay and Bisexual Resource Group (HLGBRG), which is made up of what they term 'out' gay and lesbian officers. This organisation supports colleagues and acts as a resource for the whole constabulary.

Blackbourn (2006) does provide a note of caution, however, suggesting that the overall picture is patchy, with some forces unable to challenge the deep prejudices held by some police officers. He found that some managers in the police were unable or unwilling to resist homophobia, and that homophobic incidents within the police were not properly recorded. Racist language was treated seriously, but incidents of homophobic and sexist language were not treated as disciplinary matters to the same extent. The best practice of some constabularies was not consistently replicated at a national level.

REFLECTIVE TASK

Media representations

The recent history of the media representation of gay men and lesbians is not a particularly happy one. The few gay characters portrayed often perpetuate stereotypes, rather than challenging them by presenting fully rounded personalities. This representation can range from the exaggerated mannerisms of John Inman in Are You Being Served? *to the connection between homosexuality and murderous deviance in* Silence of the Lambs.

This has changed in recent years and the best example of both positive and nuanced representation of gay men and lesbians in a police programme is in the HBO drama, The Wire. *One of the main police officer characters, Kima Greggs, is a lesbian and this is presented as simply part of her character. She is shown in work, family and social settings in a similar way to the other characters, and the challenges of adopting a child and maintaining a relationship with a non-police partner are portrayed throughout the show. She is also shown as having to deal with a sometimes hostile police culture. Omar Little, a charismatic criminal, is a gay man and one of the central characters of the show. Again, he is portrayed in a rounded, non-stereotypical way, with his sexual orientation presented as integral to his character but not his only feature. American President Barack Obama has described Omar Little as one of his favourite fictional characters.*

- *Can you think of other positive or negative representations of gay men or lesbians in films or television programmes, particularly police programmes?*

- *Do you think that changes in society's attitudes lead to changes in media representations, or is it the other way around?*

Hate crime

In a similar way to the approach taken to other aspects of hate crime, the police have adopted a subjective, victim-centred approach to homophobic hate crime. If the victim perceives that the attack on them was motivated by homophobic hatred, this must be recorded by the police. Experience in both the USA and the UK has shown that there are a number of indicators relating to the context of an attack that can identify it as homophobic, including the venue of the attack or abusive comments made by the perpetrator (Chakraborti and Garland, 2009). There does still remain some level of mistrust between the gay community and the police, which is perhaps connected to the previous history of the criminal justice system, but this situation does seem to be improving, not least because of the efforts of the GPA. Various recent research reports have shown that the police role in investigating homophobic crime is being viewed more positively and police officers are slowly acquiring a reputation for treating victims sympathetically (Chakraborti and Garland, 2009).

REFLECTIVE TASK

Policy into practice

Blackbourn (2006) uses the phrase 'policy rich but practice poor' to describe the response of some forces to homophobia.

- *What do you understand by that phrase?*

- *What is your view of the suggestion that some police forces might be better at developing policies on LGB issues than at actually improving the situation for their employees and the community?*

C H A P T E R S U M M A R Y

In this chapter you will have considered how recent a development it is that sexual orientation should be regarded as one of the six key strands of diversity. Within criminology, sexual orientation has been a marginal concern, and there is no distinct body of research or literature that analyses crime and criminal justice from a gay perspective. Criminological research did play a role, albeit in a minor way, in the legislative changes that have seen gay and lesbian relationships becoming first decriminalised and then actually protected by law. The legislative changes have been the most significant factor in the changing relationship between the police and the gay community.

It is, generally, no longer the perception of either the gay community or the police that it is a police role to persecute or prosecute the gay community. Instead, there are now some excellent examples of effective police practice in protecting the gay community from hate crime, and police constabularies are held up as exemplars of good employment practice. Although the sight of police officers parading in uniform at Gay Pride events is becoming more familiar, it is always worth remembering that such developments are relatively recent, and that in many countries of the world it is still a police task to arrest gay men and lesbians for engaging in private, adult, consensual sexual activity.

REFERENCES

Blackbourn, D (2006) Gay rights in the police service: is the enemy still within? *Criminal Justice Matters*, 63: 1, 30.

Burke, M (1994) Homosexuality as deviance: the case of the gay police officer. *British Journal of Criminology*, 34(2): 192–203.

Chakraborti, N and Garland, J (2009) *Hate Crime: Impact, Causes and Responses*. London: Sage.

Groombridge, N (1999) Perverse criminologies: the closet of Doctor Lombroso. *Social and Legal Studies*, 8(4): 531–48.

Groombridge, N (2006) Queer theory, in McLaughlin, E and Muncie, J (eds) *The Sage Dictionary of Criminology*. London: Sage.

Martis, R (2005) Taking pride, *Police Review*, 18 March: 18–20.

Newburn, T (2008) Gay Police Association, in Newburn, T and Neyroud, P (eds) *Dictionary of Policing*. Cullompton: Willan.

Rowe, M (2008) *Introduction to Policing*. London: Sage.

Stonewall (2009) *Sexual Orientation Employer Handbook*. Available online at www.stonewall.org.uk/workplace/1473.asp (accessed 15 August 2009).

Walklate, S (2004) *Gender, Crime and Criminal Justice*. Cullompton: Willan.

FURTHER READING

Dean Blackbourn's (2006) article in *Criminal Justice Matters* presents a succinct and accessible account of the current situation with regard to sexual orientation and the police, and poses the question of whether enough change has taken place, notwithstanding the positive response to the employment practices of the police. It is also worth looking at the websites of the constabularies that have received praise for their work in this area.

USEFUL WEBSITES

www.hampshire.police.uk/Internet/ (Hampshire Constabulary)

www.stonewall.org.uk/ (Stonewall)

8 Conclusion

CHAPTER OBJECTIVES

By the end of this concluding chapter you should be able to:

- discuss the diversity material covered in the rest of this book;
- explain how discussions of equality and diversity have influenced police training;
- demonstrate knowledge of past and present police practice in relation to all six strands of diversity and show an ability to implement best practice in the future;
- demonstrate a clear understanding of the importance of equality and diversity to contemporary police practice.

LINKS TO STANDARDS

This concluding chapter provides opportunities for links with the following Skills for Justice, National Occupational Standards (NOS) for Policing and Law Enforcement 2008.

AE1.1 Maintain and develop your own knowledge, skills and competence.
CA1 Use law enforcement actions in a fair and justified way.
HA1 Manage your own resources.
HA2 Manage your own resources and professional development.

Introduction

In this final section of the book, the material from the rest of the chapters will be drawn together, summarised and reflected on. This will be done chapter by chapter, each with a chapter summary and a case study-based exercise to help you reflect on the lessons learned. The book will conclude with a final discussion of the central importance of equality and diversity to modern policing. Prior to that, however, the chapter will commence with a discussion of the recent changes and developments in police training in relation to equality and diversity.

Police education and training

It is likely that student readers of this book will be involved in police training in some way, either as serving trainee officers or undertaking a higher education (HE) or further education (FE) programme in the hope of gaining entry to a police career. It is revealing in itself that diversity and equality have now become so central to the training and education of the police, as discussions of the police's approach to diversity are usually linked to recommendations for training. In this section this will be discussed, highlighting two main challenges that have been faced in this training: the difficulty in teaching the concept of institutional racism and the need to encourage self-reflection.

Initial police training was reorganised in 2006 with the introduction of the Initial Police Learning and Development Programme (IPLDP). This replaced the previous training practice of relying on regional training centres, and instead gave responsibility to local forces to provide training to meet the needs of their own communities. Many forces have entered into partnerships with local FE or HE institutions to deliver the academic element of the programme, either as part of the IPLDP, or prior to entry to the police offering later exemption (Bradley, 2009). Training in diversity, equality and community engagement is integral to the IPLDP and the police meet diversity training targets by focusing on the six strands discussed in this book, and breaking them down into the competencies required to meet the National Occupational Standards (NOS). Bryant et al. (2006, p63) describe the aim of diversity training:

> The aim of diversity training within the police service is usually to help you to meet the expectations of the public you serve and of your organization regarding your attitude and behaviour towards other people and members of diverse communities.

Diversity training in the IPLDP and throughout the organisation is influenced by the report of the Lawrence Inquiry (Macpherson, 1999) and its recommendations about police training, including that all officers should be trained in combating racism and in diversity awareness. The police have responded to this by both including diversity training in the initial training programme and running particular specialist programmes and courses. However, although taking this approach does embed diversity awareness into the training programmes, it does so at the risk of encouraging officers to treat diversity as behaviour driven and to simply learn to watch what they say, rather than undertake a genuine process of reflecting on and examining their beliefs and behaviours (Crisp and Ward, 2008).

Training in the subject of institutional racism has been particularly difficult, for two main reasons. First, there is not yet a clear understanding, in society or in the police, of what the term means, so it is therefore hard to teach. Second, the concept is still sensitive and politically charged and it can create tensions in the classroom; these tensions sometimes lead to trainers choosing to avoid the subject. This results in diversity being solely taught and understood at the level of the individual, rather than the institution or organisation (Rowe and Garland, 2007).

Wider challenges in police training also affect the teaching of diversity. So much of police work is so practical, and so demanding of swift responses to unpredictable situations, that it is tempting for police officers to assume that little that is taught in the classroom (either in police training or in FE or HE programmes prior to entry) can be relevant to the actual work of police officers on the street. This idea is reinforced by the seemingly low status given to police trainers within the organisation; they tend to be employed at practitioner grade and have little responsibility for developing the material that is to be taught (Bradley, 2009). Practical skills are often perceived – by trainees, trainers and managers – to be more important than theoretical skills, and there is a risk that this attitude could diminish the impact of diversity training. It is possible that trainees and students might perceive diversity training as simply another management imperative, and another classroom-based activity that has little relevance to 'real police work'. This can be addressed, in some way, by including community representatives in the training, and there is evidence that doing this does increase its effectiveness (Rowe and Garland, 2007).

Managers can have an even more negative impact if they explicitly or implicitly convey a message that diversity training is trivial and unimportant, or is simply about not causing offence and creating trouble for the organisation. The focus on responding to managerial imperatives means that students are even sometimes suspicious of the motives of their trainers – in the most extreme instances, expressing concern that diversity sessions might be bugged to identify officers who use inappropriate language (Rowe and Garland, 2007). A high-profile example of possibly counter-productive diversity training was seen in the documentary *The Secret Policeman*, where the footage (presumably selectively edited) seemed to show that diversity training amounted to little more than instructing officers not to use certain offensive words, with no attempt to encourage explanation of this, or to promote self-reflection.

Bryant et al. (2006) expand on the aim of diversity training quoted above by encouraging police students to go beyond meeting organisational and community expectations, and to set objectives to actually personally accept the diversity precepts. This approach would address many of the problems and concerns expressed above, but it has not always been easy to achieve.

REFLECTIVE TASK

Self-reflection

Think back over the reading and learning on diversity that you have done so far, in this book, in the associated reading and in any training you have received.

- *Has any of it changed your thinking about any aspect of diversity?*

- *Which of the six strands have you found it most challenging to consider?*

- *Have you been able to discuss diversity issues, and particularly your response to them, with colleagues or fellow students, and has this been easy or difficult?*

Revisiting the six strands of diversity

In this section the main points of the previous six chapters will be considered, along with a final case study-based exercise to help you reflect on your learning.

Age

Chapter summary

- Legislation now protects against age-based discrimination in all aspects of employment.

- Throughout the history of the criminal justice system, and throughout the world, it has been a challenge to deal appropriately with the behaviour of young children, and this is now dealt with extensively in national and international legislation.

- Many aspects of the government's respect and anti-social behaviour agendas have particular impact on young people.

- Elder abuse often goes undetected but has a serious impact on its victims.

- Despite the main legislation taking quite a coercive approach to work with young people, there are many examples of positive and restorative engagement by the police.

REFLECTIVE TASK

You are a police officer attending a community group and a few local residents raise a concern about young people hanging around outside the front door of a 24-hour supermarket at night. They say that they are too intimidated to use the shop because of the presence of this group. You know this area well and have spoken to the young people, who say that they congregate there because it is bright and safe and they have nowhere else to go. The supermarket manager has told you he would prefer the young people to go somewhere else, but they have never actually caused any trouble and he has never seen them either drinking alcohol or trying to purchase alcohol.

- *How do you respond to the residents in the group?*

Disability

Chapter summary

- There is strong legislative employment protection for people with disabilities and this includes two aspects particular to this strand of diversity. First, people with disabilities are entitled to reasonable adjustment. Second, it is legally permissible to discriminate positively in favour of people with disabilities.

- The concept of social construction is helpful in understanding all strands of diversity, but is of particular use in relation to disability.

- HIV/AIDS is a particular issue in the prison system, but has an impact on policing as well.

- The policing of disability hate crime has recently come to national attention and it is likely that the police will focus much more on this issue in the coming months and years.

- The police have clear national guidelines relating to the employment and support of staff with disabilities.

REFLECTIVE TASK

You are a police trainer who is staffing a stall at a recruitment event and you are approached by a man who says that his 18-year-old daughter is very keen to join the police, but is not sure whether she would be accepted because of her disability.

- *How would you advise this man?*

- *What questions would you need to ask about the nature of the disability before you could feel confident that you could give a full answer?*

Gender

Chapter summary

- There has long been legislative protection against discrimination in employment, and legislation providing protection from domestic abuse is more recent.

- It is only relatively recently that women have been considered as offenders within the criminal justice system; their more traditional involvement has been as victims or witnesses. There have been difficulties with how women have been treated by the criminal justice system in all these roles.

- It has been challenging for women to gain equal employment rights in recruitment and selection in society, and this has also been the case in the police. The police culture is still perceived as male-dominated and 'macho'.

- The increase in the number of women employed by the police has been a factor in the improvement in practice in dealing with offences against women and children, although there is still progress that needs to be made. There is, however, a risk that female police officers might find themselves disproportionately encouraged into working with these offences, with a possible detrimental effect on their careers.

- Much attention has been paid to gender and policing in the future and there is guidance available to promote best practice, including the Corston Report and the Gender Agenda.

REFLECTIVE TASK

You are a police officer and you call at a flat in response to a report that a serious sexual assault has taken place. It quickly becomes clear that the young woman who has made the call has been drinking alcohol and the alleged offender (who is not now present) is her ex-boyfriend, whom she had met in a pub and invited back to her flat.

- *What are your immediate assumptions?*

- *From this initial, limited information, which has revealed nothing about the alleged offence itself, have you formed a view about the likelihood of a conviction in this case?*

Race

Chapter summary

- The Macpherson Report dominates all discussions of race and policing and is also a key document in considering any aspect of diversity in relation to both the police and society in general.

- Legislation protects against racial discrimination in employment and the provision of services, and there is also strong protection against racially motivated hate crime.

- The correct use of language is a highly charged, complicated and emotive issue and there is not always clear consensus on which terms are correct. It is vital, however, that police staff make every effort to use correct terminology and understand that misuse of language can cause real hurt and offence.

- The whole criminal justice system has struggled to deal well with issues of race, with the police and prisons having a particularly poor record. It is important to remember that victims, offenders and the public often perceive the criminal justice system as one entity, so the good or bad practice of one agency can affect individuals' experience of the whole system.

- The police have made a lot of positive progress in the last decade, and have particularly improved their practice with regard to hate crime and in the commitment of the force's national and local leaders.

- Work still needs to be done in creating a more diverse workforce, representative of the community it serves, and in gaining the community's confidence in the use of stop and search powers and the DNA database.

REFLECTIVE TASK

You are attending a diversity training session for police staff, which is being delivered in an interdisciplinary way – the group includes students, administrators, police officers, PCSOs and a few sergeants and inspectors. As far as you can tell, there are only three people in the group of about 40 who are black or Asian. All the trainers are white men. The trainers deliver the material fairly professionally but occasionally use phrases such as 'political correctness' or 'the problem of race', which makes you feel slightly unsure of their commitment to the material they are delivering. You have also become aware, as the day has gone on, that there is an Asian woman, who you know to be a PCSO but do not know personally, who is looking increasingly uncomfortable and does not appear to be talking to anyone throughout the day.

- *What response can you make to this situation?*

- *Is there anything you can or should do to support your colleague?*

- *Is the behaviour of the trainers acceptable and is there any action you should take?*

- *If you decide to do nothing, what would that mean in relation to the importance of good diversity training and to the responsibility of every individual officer?*

Religion

Chapter summary

- The legislative anomalies that led to some religions, but not all, being protected under race discrimination legislation have now largely been resolved.

- A religious identity can be either a statement of strong belief or a looser cultural association, and both are entitled to protection.

- The police must pay particular attention to Islam because of the need to protect Muslims from hate crime and the need to protect society from extremist-led terrorism.

- The religious make-up of the Police Service of Northern Ireland (PSNI) has been addressed through proactive recruitment processes, and this has impacted on the organisation itself and its relationship with the community.

- Religiously aggravated offences currently have a very high profile due to both factors in society and changes in legislation. It is vital that the police respond sensitively and appropriately.

- A number of religious associations have been formed to provide support and advocacy for police staff associated with particular religious groups.

You are a PCSO and you receive a report of trouble between two groups of young people. You go to investigate, with a colleague, and while you speak to a group of white young people, he speaks to a group of Asian young people. The group tells you that there was no real trouble, just a few words exchanged. Your colleague confirms that the young people he spoke to say the same thing, so you send the group of white young people away, and join your colleague with the other group. They report to you that what actually happened was that they were returning from the mosque when they were subjected to unprovoked abuse from the other group, including some very offensive terms. They report that this happens every week and they are concerned that it might escalate into violence at some stage.

- *How do you persuade the group that you will take their concerns seriously?*

- *What practical steps could the police take to make them feel safe?*

- *What will you say to your colleague, who seems to have treated the group's concerns quite dismissively?*

Sexual orientation

Chapter summary

- Legal protection against discrimination on the basis of sexual orientation is relatively recent, but there is now strong protective legislation that also covers hate crime, as well as creating a legal basis for civil partnerships.

- The relationship between the gay community and the police has changed dramatically in the last few decades. The police used regularly to devote resources to detecting consensual sexual activity, but they are now identified by Stonewall as an exemplary employer.

- Hate crime against gay men and lesbians remains a problem, particularly in some regions, but the police are gaining skill and confidence in responding to it.

- The police need to ensure that the strong policy framework is matched by consistent good practice.

As a police officer, you call to the house of a woman who has reported an act of vandalism against her property. You interview her with her nine-year-old son, and she explains that she has experienced a lot of both vandalism and verbal abuse from people in the area, particularly at times when her partner is away from home because of work. She has never reported anything before because each individual incident is a minor one, and she was worried about making the situation worse, but she now feels that she needs to act as her son is becoming increasingly distressed. During the course of the conversation it becomes clear that her partner is a woman, and she is in a same-sex relationship.

- *How could you respond to this complainant?*

- *If you suspected that this pattern of behaviour amounted to homophobic hate crime, what evidence would you need to confirm this?*

- *What difference would it make to how you would proceed?*

Equality and diversity in policing

It is hoped that, having read this far, you will no longer require to be convinced of the importance of equality and diversity in twenty-first-century policing. The summaries above highlight both the common themes that run across all six strands of diversity and the particular approach that is required in relation to each of them. However, at this final point of the book it is worth reinforcing this message by considering what the most influential recent review of policing, known as the Flanagan Review (Flanagan, 2008), has to say on the subject.

- Improving staff development and promoting greater flexibility in working practices should lead to the creation of a more diverse workforce.

- Lessons should be learned from the positive work done in creating a diverse workforce at PCSO grade. It may be that the greater opportunity for community involvement in this role is attractive to women and applicants from ethnic minorities.

- Neighbourhood policing has an important role to play in promoting community cohesion.

- It is important that police forces are accountable to both inspectors and police authorities in the progress they make against diversity targets.

Although the six strands are not considered in detail, the message of the review echoes the themes of this book, summarised above, that promoting diversity relates both to the police organisation and to the interaction between the police and the public. It is central to the identity and function of the police, and individual officers and entire forces can, rightly, expect to be held to account for their practice in this regard. The contemporary approach is increasingly to widen the discussion so that diversity is no longer solely discussed primarily in relation to race, but relates to the six strands and even beyond them to such issues as poverty, immigration status, language and homelessness (Rowe, 2004).

The title of this book is *Equality and Diversity*, and most of the focus of the discussion has been on diversity. It is worth giving some final attention to the issue of equality, however, as it is an important part of the debate. The language of diversity has largely overtaken the language of equal opportunities in the criminal justice system, as diversity is perceived to be a more positive approach and equal opportunities are associated with the inadequate approach of simply treating everyone the same. However, it is worth noting that promoting diversity in itself does not necessarily create a more equal society.

A focus on diversity alone can actually have the effect of neglecting society's inequalities and therefore perpetuating them (Orr, 2009). Most, if not all, of the problems that face society, such as drug abuse, offending and family breakdown, are closely linked to inequality (Wilkinson and Pickett, 2009), so it is vital that consideration of diversity also includes the promotion of greater equality. The work of the EHRC, and the likely enactment of the single Equality Bill in 2010, will continue to bring discussions of diversity and equality closer together. The role of the police will continue to be central to the creation of a fair, diverse and equal society.

Throughout this book, examples from practice have been used to illustrate the points made. Many of these examples have been fictional ones (or real examples with changes made to key details), but some have been true examples taken from media reports, including some very recent examples from 2009. The policing and diversity context changes whenever a particular incident receives national attention, and it is therefore easy to predict that the police will deal with new and unpredictable diversity issues in the months and years ahead. The likely enactment of the Equality Bill will change both the legislative and policy context. However, it is hoped that honest self-reflection on the issues discussed here, along with adherence to the principles of best diversity practice, will allow police students and police practitioners in all roles to continue to promote diversity equality both within the organisation and in the police's interaction with the public.

REFERENCES

Bradley, D (2009) Education and training, in Wakefield, A and Fleming, J (eds) *The Sage Dictionary of Policing*. London: Sage.

Bryant, R, Caless, B, Lawton-Barrett, K, Underwood, R and Wood, D (2006) *Blackstone's Student Police Officer Handbook*. Oxford: Oxford University Press.

Crisp, A and Ward, D (2008) Policing the community in the 21st century, in Stout, B, Yates, J and Williams, B (eds) *Applied Criminology*. London: Sage.

Flanagan, R (2008) *The Review of Policing*. London: Home Office.

Macpherson, Sir W (1999) *The Stephen Lawrence Inquiry*. London: HMSO.

Orr, D (2009) Diversity and equality are not the same thing, *The Guardian*. Available online at: www.guardian.co.uk/commentisfree/2009/oct/22/diversity-equality-deborah-orr (accessed 15 August 2009).

Rowe, M (2004) *Policing, Race and Racism*. Cullompton: Willan.

Rowe, M and Garland, J (2007) Police diversity training: a silver bullet tarnished?, in Rowe, M (ed.) *Policing Beyond Macpherson: Issues in Policing, Race and Society*. Cullompton: Willan.

Wilkinson, R and Pickett, K (2009) *The Spirit Level: Why Equal Societies Almost Always Do Better*. London: Allen Lane.

Michael Rowe and Jon Garland's chapter on police diversity training in *Beyond Macpherson* (ed. Rowe, 2007) covers all the key issues and challenges in providing diversity training to the police during the past decade. Richard Wilkinson and Kate Pickett's *The Spirit Level* (2009) makes a compelling case for the importance of promoting a more equal society and the impact that would have.

Index

Note that material in task boxes has often been included in the following index.

Policing Matters

Equality and Diversity in Policing